From Sue
Xmas '83

Wine Tour

SONOMA & MENDOCINO

Jeffrey Caldewey

A Vintage Image Book

COPYRIGHT © 1982 VINTAGE IMAGE. NO PORTION OF THIS BOOK MAY BE REPRODUCED IN WHOLE OR IN PART WITHOUT THE PERMISSION OF THE PUBLISHER. PUBLISHED IN THE UNITED STATES BY VINTAGE IMAGE, 1335 MAIN ST., ST. HELENA, CA 94574
ISBN: 0-918666-19-8. LIB. OF CONGRESS CAT. NO. 79-53698.

Table of Contents

SOUTHERN SONOMA VALLEY WINERIES MAP	9
SONOMA TOWN MAP	11
CENTRAL SONOMA COUNTY WINERIES MAP	13
SANTA ROSA TOWN MAP	15
NORTHERN SONOMA COUNTY WINERIES MAP	17
HEALDSBURG TOWN MAP	19
MENDOCINO COUNTY WINERIES MAP	21
UKIAH TOWN MAP	23
FOOD — reviews of restaurants and provenders, geographically listed south to north	24
RESTAURANT MENUS — the vintner's choice	39
LODGING — reviews of lodgings and accomodations, geographically listed south to north	50
WINERY INDEX — vital winemaking and visitor information, alphabetically listed	64

California
Oregon
Nevada
Pacific Ocean
Arizona
Mexico

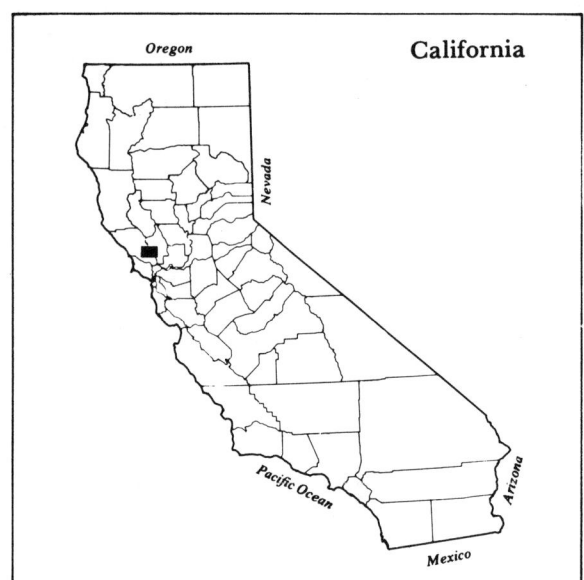

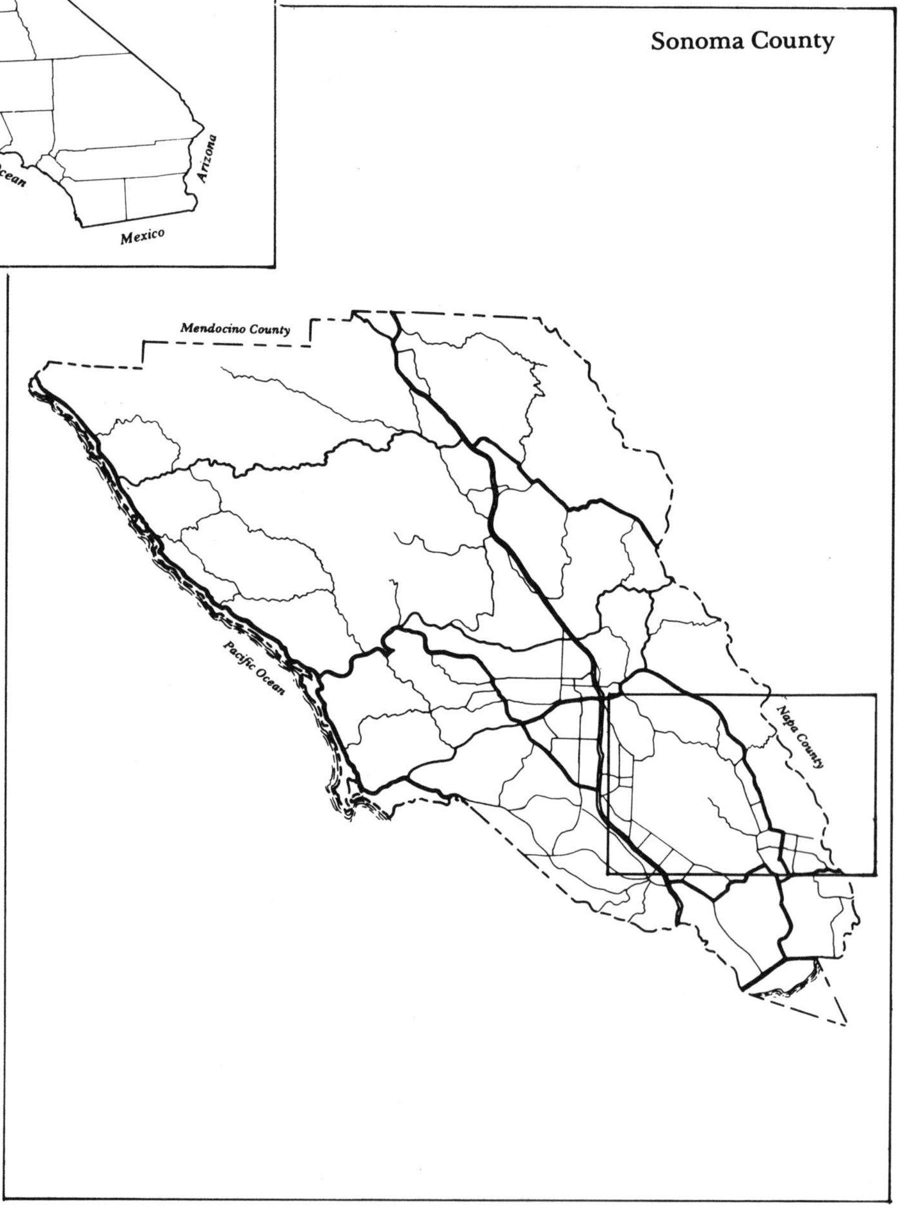
Sonoma County
Mendocino County
Pacific Ocean
Napa County

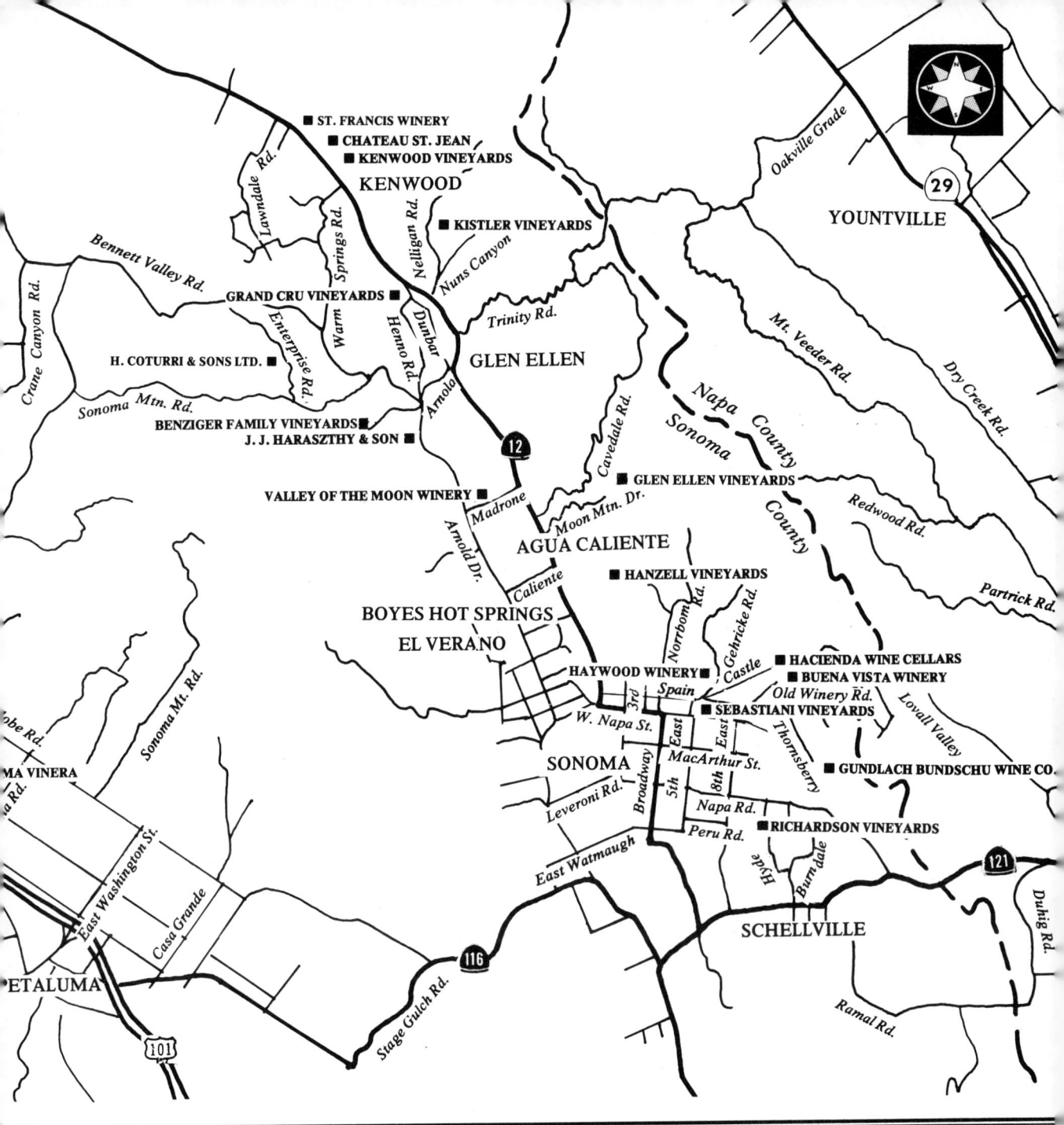

Southern Sonoma Wineries

CITY OF SONOMA
A PERSPECTIVE

Sonoma County has been an exciting and beautiful land since time began. The dramatic contrast of rugged coast and expansive plains, towering mountains and fertile valleys has been attracting wayfarers for hundreds of years.

The Indians, Pomo, Miwok and Wappo, lived here for thousands of years in virtual paradise. The weather was mild, the streams full with fish, there was plenty of game and the land abounded in roots, seeds and acorns. The word Sonoma is derived from the Suisun language, and translates "vale of many moons."

Much of California's early history was made in Sonoma. It was in turn Indian land, home of the Suisuns and Soto Yomes; a mission settlement; a pueblo; a presidio and northern outpost on which seven different flags were flown-Spain, England, Russia, Mexican Empire, Mexican Republic, California Republic and finally the stars and stripes of the United States.

The last of twenty-one missions was founded here by Fra. Jose Altimira who blessed the spot on July 4, 1823. A chapel was completed the following year and 1000 vines were planted.

Sonoma Valley is considered "the birthplace of California viniculture." Here, ten years after the padres planted their vines, Don Mariano Guadalupe Vallejo set out vines other than the mission variety in 1834.

Haraszthy, "the father of California viticulture," imported 100,000 grape cuttings of 140 varieties and became head of the Buena Vista Vinicultural Society, in possession of 5,100 acres of land, 362,000 grapevines and six mountainside cellars, each 125 feet long.

By 1875, Sonoma County produced more wine, by far, than any other county in California. Haraszthy's favorite zinfandel vine was the most widely planted grape variety in California by 1900.

Sonoma Valley resident Jack London romanticized Sonoma in his novel, "The Valley of the Moon," and spread the word about this unique and beautiful spot. In 1961 the United States government issued the proclamation designating the historic buildings and grounds of the Sonoma Plaza area as a national monument.

Today the Sonoma Plaza is a visitors headquarters where people enjoy picnics, meet friends and delight in the huge shade trees perched on the expansive lawn. Many people enjoy the historic buildings including the restored Toscano Hotel, the barracks (newly restored), Spanish and Mexican adobes, Mission San Francisco de Solano, and the Vasquez house, built by Col. Joseph Hooker which can be admired across the street near the complex of small shops.

The many unique restaurants facing the Square offer elegance in dining and support the claim that the finest wine growing areas of the world also possess the most superior cuisine. Good wine and good food go hand-in-hand here.

The Valley also offers guests the delightful towns of Boyes Hot Springs, Fetters Hot Springs, Glen Ellen, Agua Caliente and Kenwood. This favored recreational region has a championship 18-hole golf course, many swimming pools, riding trails, football and baseball fields, tennis courts, state parks and of course the historic wineries.

Sonoma Valley

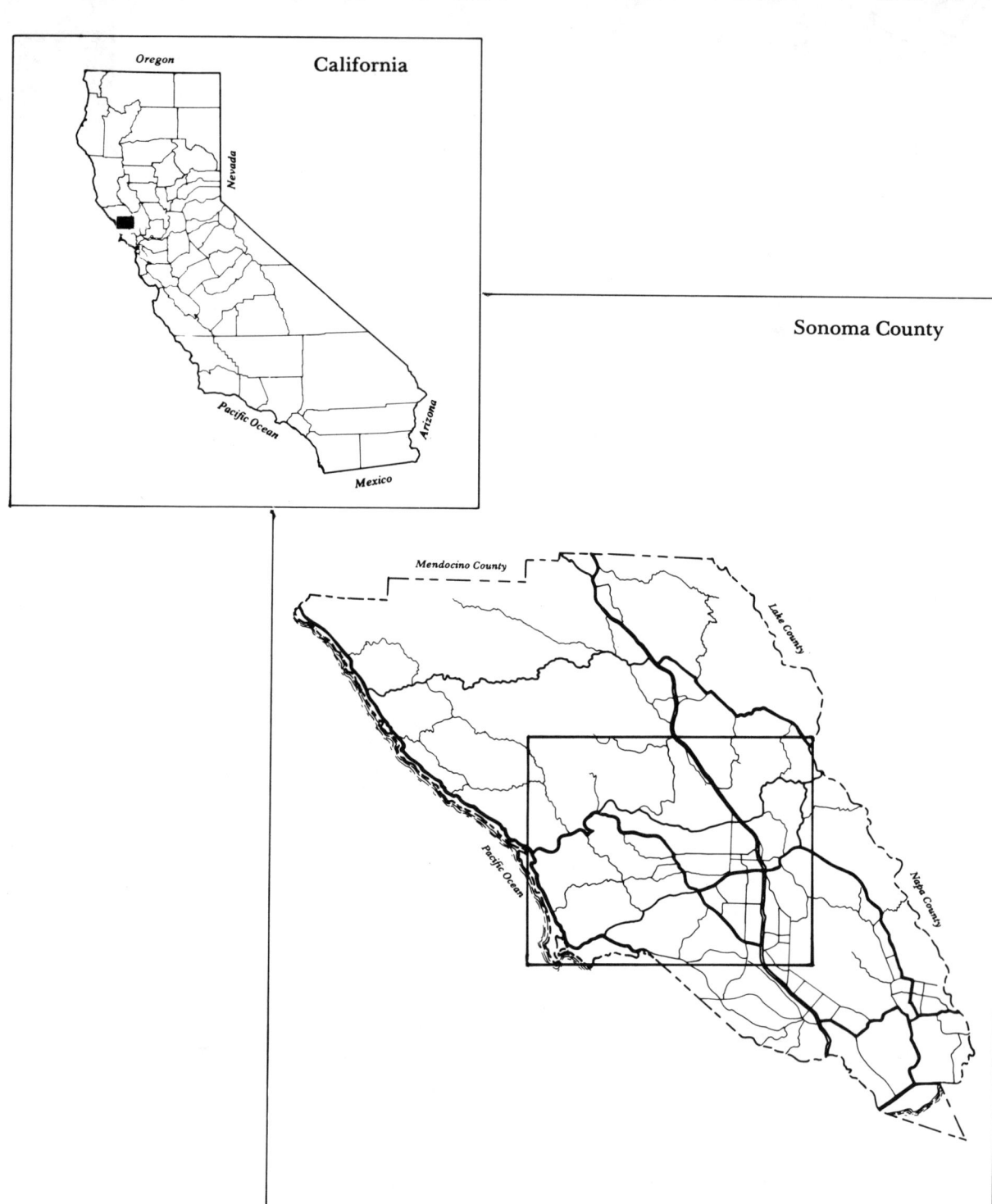

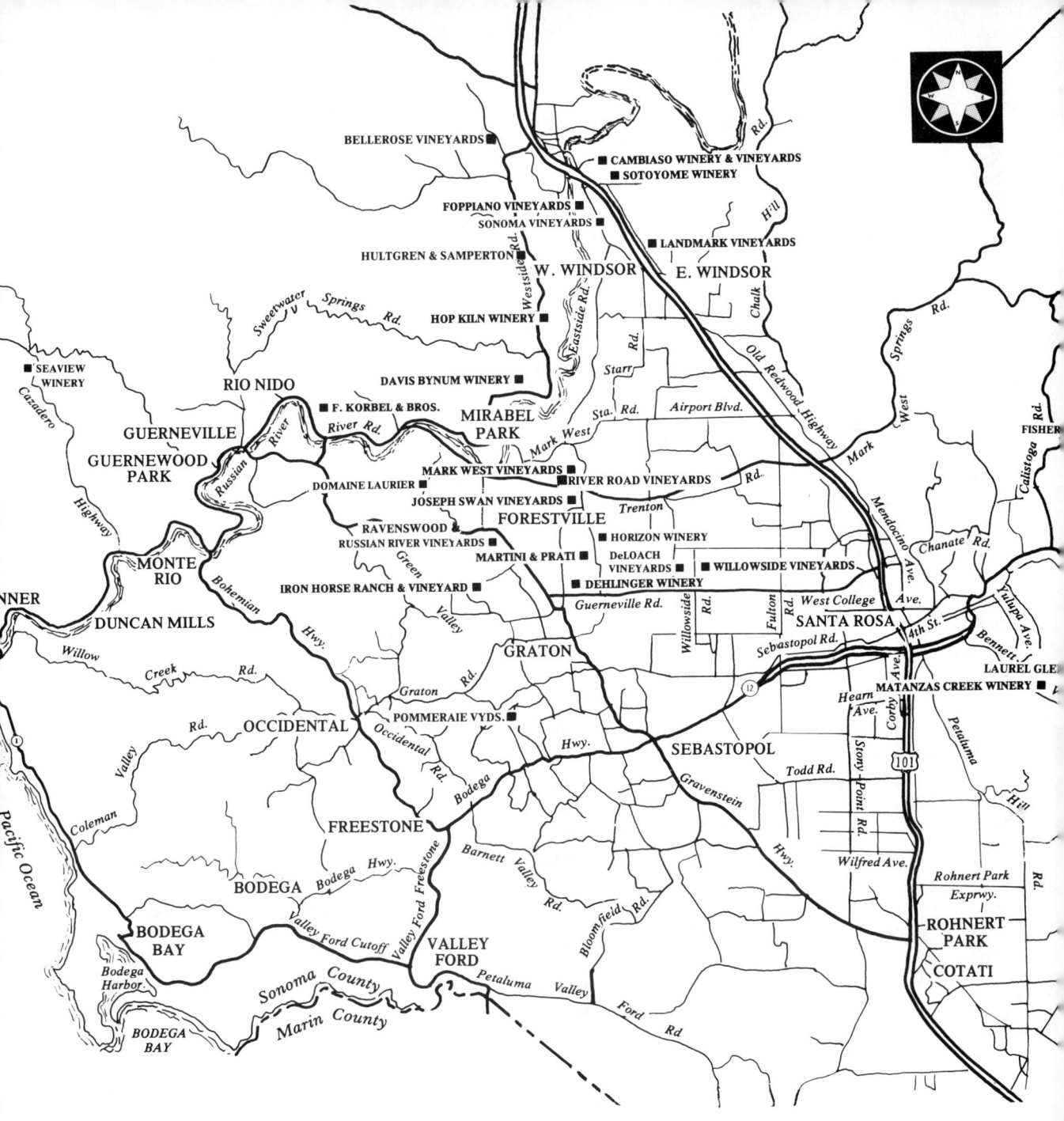

Central Sonoma Wineries

CITY OF SANTA ROSA
A PERSPECTIVE

Father Juan Amoroso founded the mission of San Rafael and then traveled north to give the beautiful name of Santa Rosa to an area he toured in 1829. While baptizing a young Indian woman in a stream during his expedition, hostile Indians attacked and forced the priest and his companion Jose Cantua to hurriedly mount their horses and escape. This happened on the day the church celebrates the Feast of St. Rosa of Lima, said to be the only canonized woman saint of the new world. Consequently Father Amoroso named the stream from the incident, the stream named the Valley, and throughout the years this town of Santa Rosa has grown and attracted many colorful residents.

General Mariano Guadalupe Vallejo was sent by the Mexican government to Santa Rosa in 1833. He arranged for Rancho Cabeza de Santa Rosa to be founded by his mother-in-law Senora Carillo, and became the first permanent settlement in the valley.

The Bear Flag Revolt in 1846 brought American settlers and a trading post to Santa Rosa, and the county seat followed in 1854 when Old Peg Leg Menefee stole the court house records in Sonoma and after a wild buckboard ride behind a team of horses, delivered them to the town fathers of Santa Rosa.

Luther Burbank remains one of the most lustrous citizens of Santa Rosa. His home and gardens are now a national monument and this world famous horticultural scientist described Santa Rosa, best of all . . . "I firmly believe from all that I have seen that this is the chosen spot of all the Earth as far as nature is concerned. The climate is perfect . . . The air so sweet that it is a pleasure to drink it in . . . The sunshine so pure and soft; the mountains which gird the Valley are lovely. The Valley is covered with majestic oaks placed as no human hand could arrange them for beauty . . . Great rose trees climb over the houses, loaded with every color of blossoms . . . I almost have to cry for joy when I look at the lovely panorama from the hillside." (1875)

Santa Rosa was badly damaged during the 1906 earthquake. The town was rebuilt and thanks to resident Frank P. Doyle, "Father of the Golden Gate Bridge," the town became more closely linked to San Francisco in 1937.

Today Santa Rosa, named "The City Designed For Living," is the largest city in Sonoma County with a population of 66,400 as of January 1, 1976.

Its 26½ square miles contain Robert L. Ripley's world famous church of one tree, golf courses, numerous swimming facilities, tennis, theaters, parks, one of the west's largest shopping centers, excellent hotels, motels and restaurants.

Santa Rosa is the gateway to the Redwood Empire. Located 47 miles north of the Golden Gate Bridge, 100 miles west of Sacramento, 446 miles north of Los Angeles and 21 miles from the Pacific Ocean. The town is surrounded by beautiful vineyards and orchards and has been described as the fastest growing area in the San Francisco Bay region.

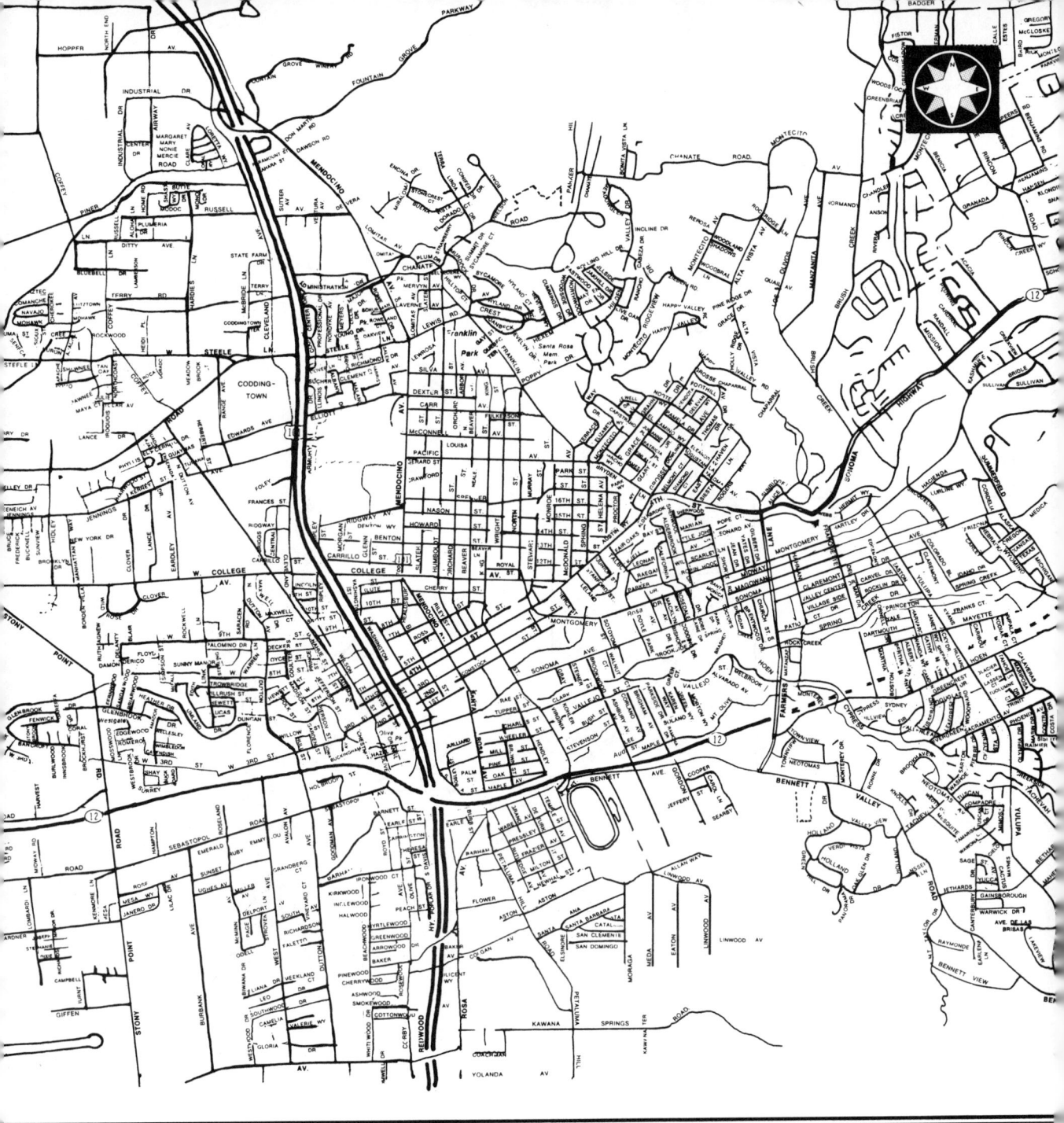

Santa Rosa

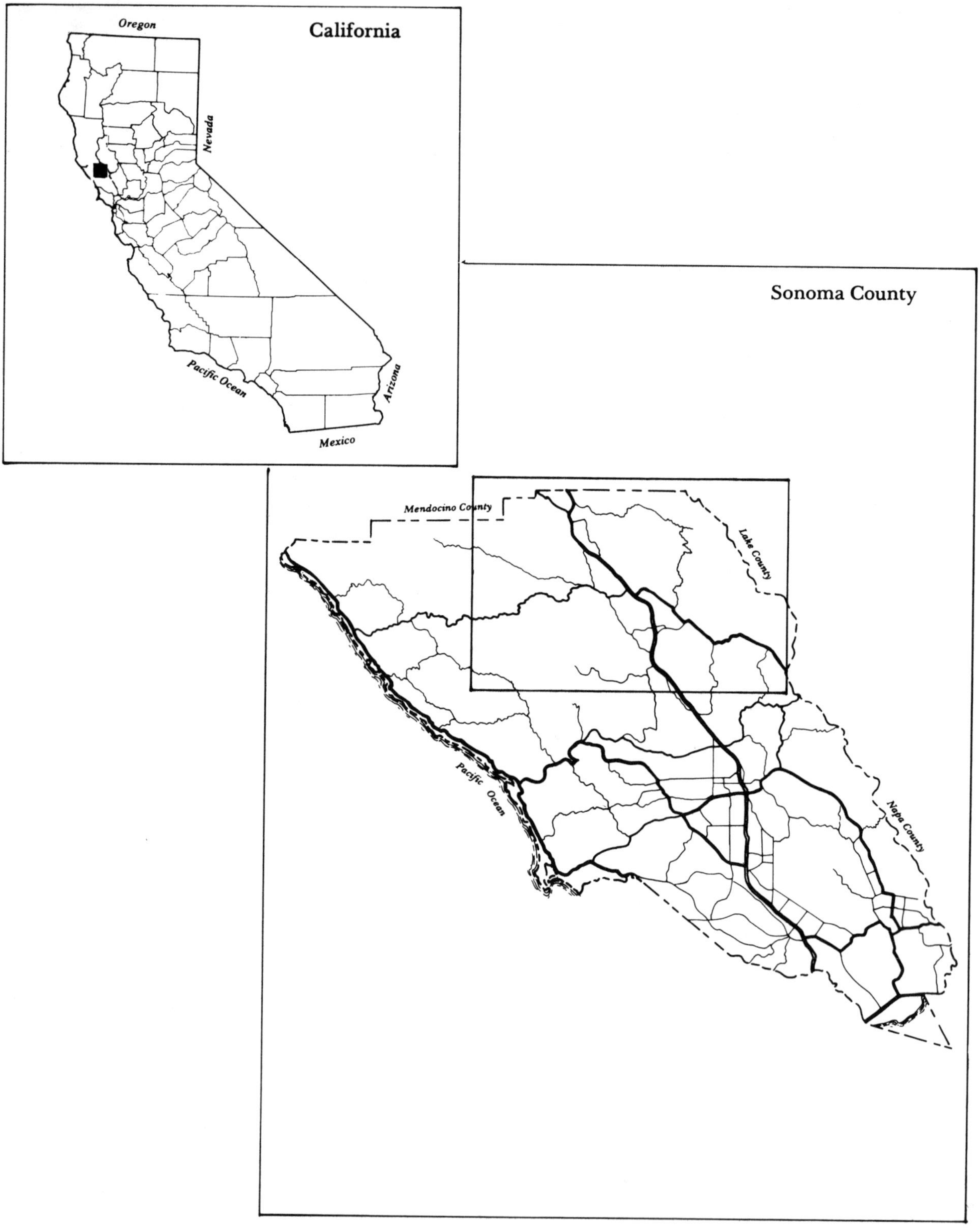

California

Sonoma County

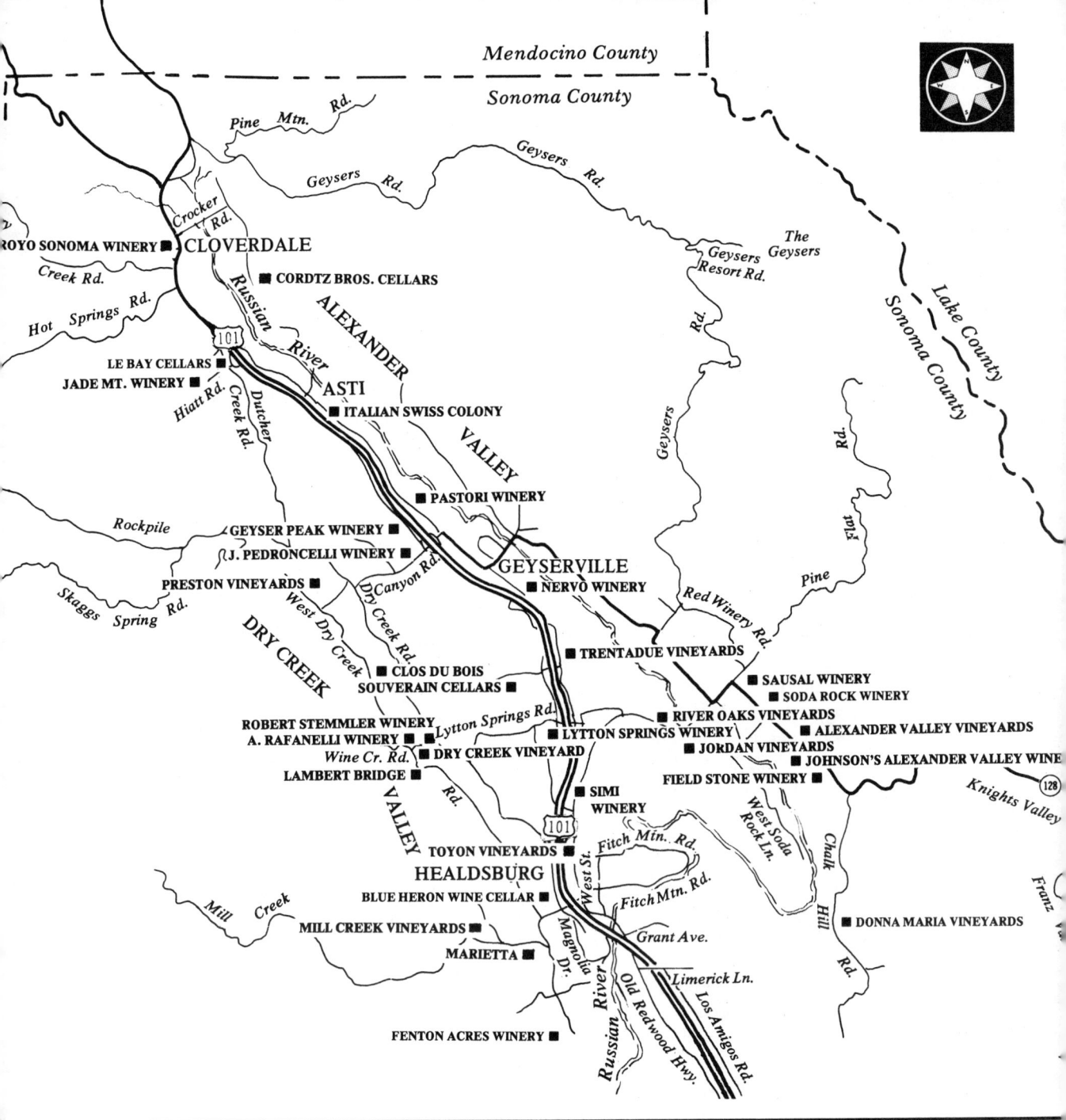

Northern Sonoma Wineries

CITY OF HEALDSBURG
PERSPECTIVE

The town of Healdsburg is part of the Sotoyome grant originally given by the Mexican government to Captain Henry Fitch. The romantic episode linked with his name is one of the great legends of the area.

The young American sailor first arrived in California in 1826, soon to be captured by the charms of Josefa Carrillo, daughter of Joaquin Carrillo of San Diego. She in turn was enthralled by the dashing young man. In 1827 he gave her a promise of marriage in writing, but because Fitch was a foreigner there were legal impediments. Josefa's parents approved of their plans and a Dominican friar was willing to perform the ceremony. With the utmost secrecy Captain Fitch was baptized on April 14, 1829, at a chapel in San Diego. The friar had promised to marry the couple the following day at the home of the Carrillos, but after last minute preparations, Domingo Carrillo, Josefa's uncle, refused to serve as witness and the ceremony could not proceed. The friar lost his courage despite the arguments, pleadings and tears of the young couple. All he could do was suggest to Fitch that there were other countries with less stringent laws.

Young Josefa coyly suggested that she be carried off by her husband-to-be. He approved the scheme as did her cousin, Pio Pico, even though her parents were not consulted. The very next evening Pio Pico took his cousin up on his horse with him and rode swiftly to a spot on the shore where a boat was waiting. The lovers were reunited on board ship and were married July 3, 1829, at Valparaiso.

The first white settler of Healdsburg township was Cyrus Alexander, a native of Pennsylvania. He had come to California in 1837 and at San Diego made the acquaintance of Captain Fitch, then a prominent merchant. Fitch sent Alexander north in search of land. In the valley of the Russian River he found a fertile tract meeting all the desired qualifications. Fitch made application to the Mexican authorities for the Sotoyome grant of eleven leagues of land, and there Alexander guarded his stock for four years. His payment was one half the increase plus two leagues of the grant. The land he selected, now called the Alexander Valley, is one of the principal grape growing regions of the Healdsburg area.

It was not until 1852 that Harmon Heald of Ohio located the site of the city. He erected a small cabin to the side of the main road traveling north and opened the first store. He was soon joined by other settlers and by 1857 the name Healdsburg was officially adopted.

Besides the large number of wineries in the immediate Healdsburg vicinity there are several attractions to the town. The annual Prune Blossom Tour through nearby valleys takes place in March and the Russian River Wine Fest is held on the second Saturday in May in the plaza.

Fitch Mountain, so named after Captain Fitch, is a former resort area withing one mile of downtown. The uncanny Geysers, located 1700 feet above sea level in the Mayacamas range, produce springs with healing properties long known to the Indians. Picnic facilities are located at Healdsburg Memorial Beach, the Alexander Valley Bridge Campground, and several local wineries.

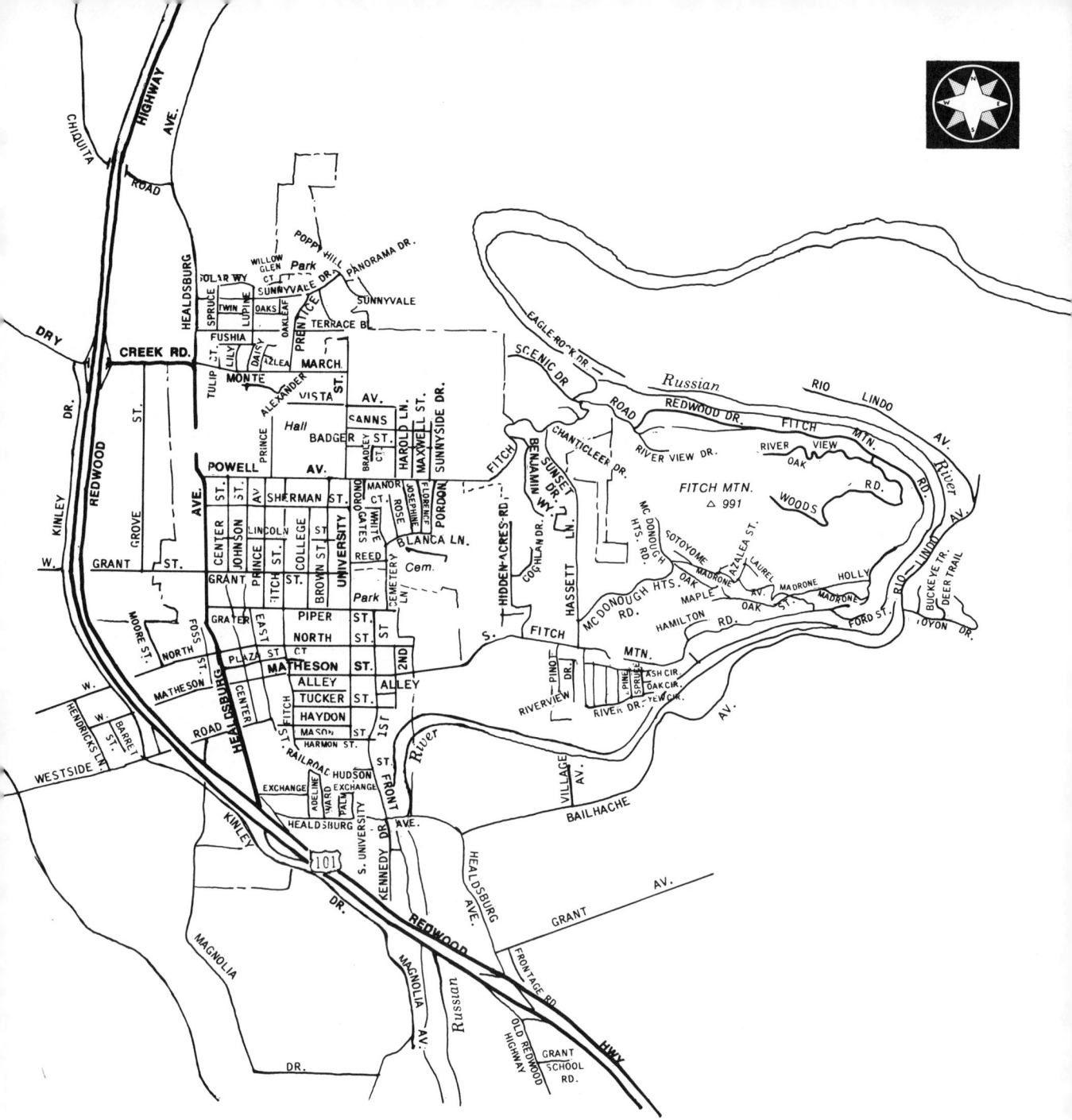

Healdsburg

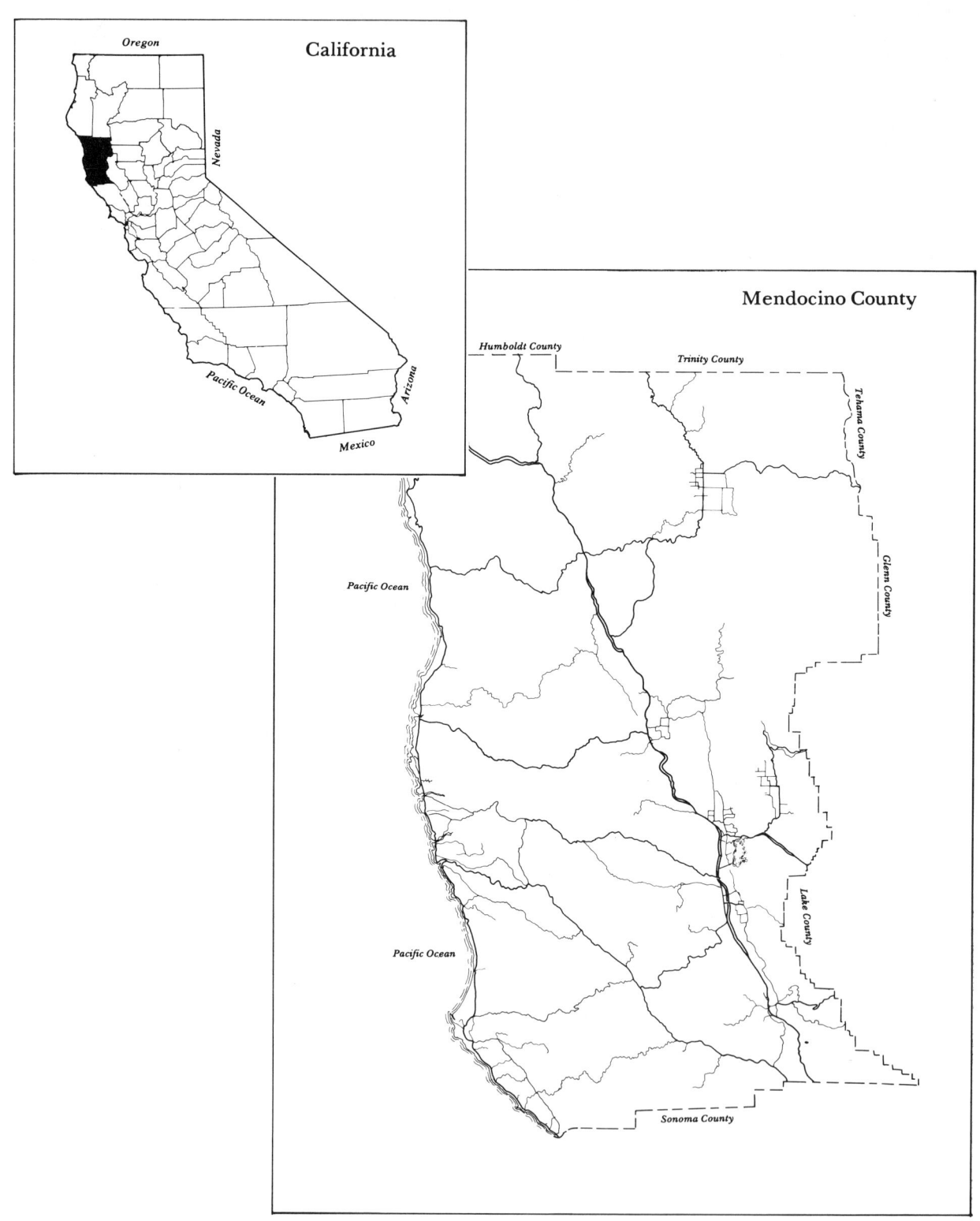

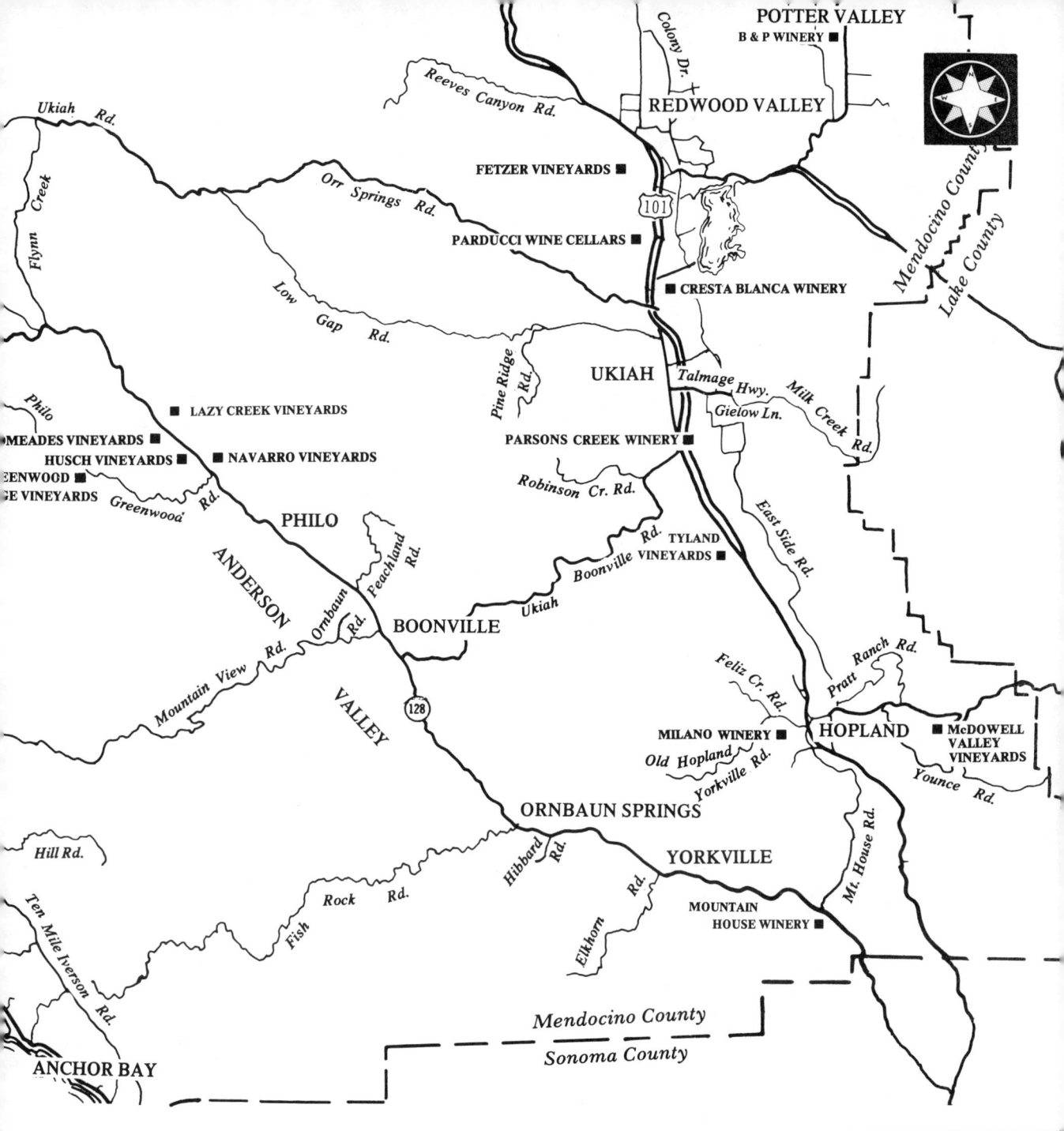

Mendocino Wineries

CITY OF UKIAH PERSPECTIVE

An independent peaceful group of the Pomos, living apart from the rest of the Central Pomo Indians, existed comfortably in Ukiah valley for many years. The abundant supplies of fish and wildlife allowed them freedom from tilling the soil. Their first interruption came in 1835 when Captain Sepulvedo Vallejo entered Mendocino County with his troops to capture Indians for work on the buildings in the town of Sonoma.

The first white man in the Ukiah valley was John Parker who arrived as an employee of James Black, a large land owner and cattle rancher of Marin County. For his sake alone, the valley was for some time referred to as the Parker Valley. The other name, Yokayo, comes from the Indian word, Yokaia, meaning south valley.

Of the two Spanish land grants covering Mendocino County, the Yokayo Grant was considered the more important. It had been given to Cayetano Juarez Pio Pico, the governor of upper California in 1845. At that time the grant covered all of Ukiah valley and the present city of Ukiah. The first settlers were impressed with the beauty of the valley, surrounded by dominant mountains, well-timbered, and bisected by the Russian River. In addition, grass was abundant for the grazing of cattle and sheep, and the soil on the valley floor was found to be particularly productive.

Those settlers who remained and contributed to the growth and development of the Ukiah area arrived between 1856 and 1857. In their search for livelihoods the planting and harvesting of grain became popular immediately due to the mild climate and fertile soil. With popularity came surplus, and grain plantings soon gave way to pears, peaches, tobacco, grapes, and hops. Again, the Pomo Indians furnished much of the labor in harvesting and processing the hops which supplanted tobacco as the major crop of the area. Spotted throughout Sonoma and Mendocino counties old hop kilns or modern buildings modeled after hop kilns are often visible along the roadside.

Grapes were first planted in the Ukiah valley in 1863, about the same time as tobacco. Originally grapes were planted purely for local consumption and because the rocky soil on the hills surrounding the valley floor was found to be suitable for grape vines. Many of the early settlers of the valley hailed from the grape regions of Italy, and both commercial grape growing and home wine production caught on as family business ventures. The first winery in Mendocino County was founded by a Prussian immigrant, Louis Finne, in 1879. By 1880, 330 acres of grapes were thriving throughout the county.

By the year 1859, Ukiah had become the prominent commerce center of Mendocino and as such was selected the county seat. Organization of government, fire department, and railroad as well as construction of bank buildings and residences was underway. Many restored landmark homes predating 1905 today line the streets of residential districts.

The large industrial plant in the Ukiah area is that of Masonite Corporation, a producer of pressed hardboard. Ten miles outside of town is the popular recreation area of Lake Mendocino.

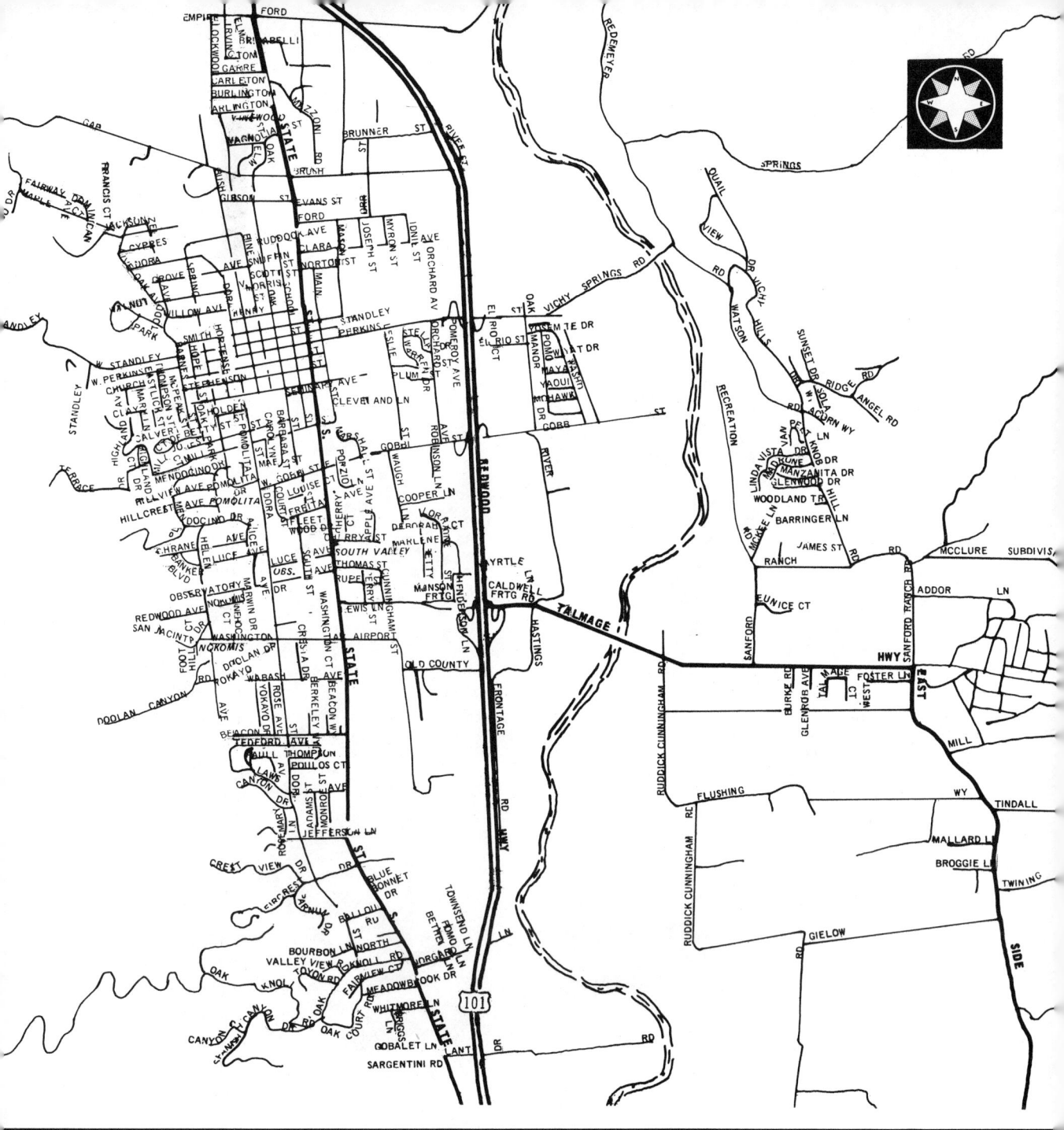

Ukiah

SONOMA

isitors to the charming rural areas of Sonoma and Mendocino Counties have an opportunity to discover numerous quaint eateries tucked away in the vineyards and redwoods. It is common knowledge, particularly among wine enthusiasts, that wine and food form a most successful and pleasurable marriage. What better way to enjoy the product of the area's sun-kissed vines than to pamper one's palate with accompanying nourishment!

This guide provides a listing of good restaurants for the hungry wine traveler. The area covered, centering around the wineries of the two counties, has a broad range; therefore, the most noteworthy establishments have been included.

The initial list of restaurants to be reviewed in this guide was compiled from the recommendations of winery personnel. The establishments were then evaluated for freshness and quality of food, atmosphere, price range, and service. The following information is intended to inform the reader of what to expect in these categories when visiting the restaurants, rather than to classify or grade them.

For those wishing to picnic, a listing of delicatessens, wine shops, and other unique shops supplying provisions is included. The Sonoma County Farm Trails map, available at local Chambers of Commerce and most winery tasting rooms, lists member farmers, processors, craftsmen, and their outlets. The detailed map locates farms which sell everything from fresh fruit to live Christmas trees. Several picnic areas and campgrounds are also marked.

EASTSIDE GRILL *Patio Cafe, Restaurant, Bar*

Just a bit off the main square, the Eastside Grill is entered through a charming brick lane. Just as you pass a tank of clamoring lobsters, the enticing aromas of mesquite charcoal and freshly grilled seafood become evident. The daily selections of seafood, game birds, or homemade pasta appear on a large blackboard. Diners can enjoy meals in the tree shaded patio—perfect for the balmy Sonoma evenings; on chilly nights, retreat into the cozy indoor dining area. The wine list is as well done as the rest of the well conceived establishment, featuring a reasonable selection from both Napa and Sonoma Valleys.

The Eastside Grill, 133 East Napa St., Sonoma 95476. Telephone: (707) 938-4909. Hours: 11:00 a.m.-11:00 p.m. Thursday-Tuesday. Price Range: Lunch $3.00-$15.00, Dinner $6.00-$20.00. Seating: 80. Full bar service. Cards: MC, VISA. No Reservations.

CAFE PILOU *Restaurant*

That Sonoma's long-awaited gastronomic rennaisance is underway is well evidenced by the opening of Cafe Pilou. Located in a quaint cobblestone courtyard bearing the name, "Place des Pyrenees" this lovely little cafe seems removed intact from a Paris street corner.

Under the tutelage of owners Linda Ives and Francoise Guerra, meals are prepared to please both the aesthetic eye as well as the palate of the gourmet. The creative menu features local produce extensively—Sonoma French Bakery bread, fertile ranch eggs, whole creamy sweet butter, garden fresh vegetables and herbs, and sausages from Sonoma Sausage Factory. All meals are accompanied by perfectly butter-sauteed pommes frites and with an obligatory cup of French roast or espresso.

Cafe Pilou, 464 First St. East Sonoma 95476 Telephone: (707) 996-2757. Hours: breakfast and Lunch: 9-2:30 Tues.-Sun., Dinner: 5:30-9:30 Thurs.-Sun. Price Range: Breakfast $2.50-$5.95, Dinner $5.95-$12.95, Corkage $3.50. Seating: 80. Reservations advises. Cards: VISA, MC.

SONOMA

SONOMA FRENCH BAKERY — *Provisions*

The Sonoma French Bakery is a shrine for genuine Sourdough French bread lovers. This is some of the finest French bread to be found in California.

Lili and Gratieu Guerra are quick to reveal their "secret ingredient" which is dedication, willingness to work hard, and concern for how the bread turns out.

The Guerra's moved to Sonoma from France in the mid-1950's. They feel their bread is as good or better than any in France. Be sure to take a number when you walk in the door.

Sonoma French Bakery, 468 First St. East, Sonoma 95476. Telephone (707) 996-2691. Hours: Wed.-Sat. 8 a.m.-6 p.m.; Sun. 7:30 a.m.-12:00 noon. French bread $.60-$1.85; also pastries and cookies.

SONOMA CHEESE FACTORY — *Provisions*

Celso Viviani, the patriarch of this cheese factory, arrived in Sonoma during 1912. He was employed by the Sonoma Mission Creamery in the early 1920's and was finally able to open his own plant with a partner in 1931. The newly-renovated Cheese Factory has been serving cheese, wine and delicatessen items since 1945 and interested visitors can view the cheese-making process. The Cheese Factory offers outdoor cafe dining, wine-tasting by the glass or taste, their famous Sonoma Jack, sandwiches to order and their catering specialty which is appropriately called the "Vintner's Buffet."

The Sonoma Cheese Factory, 2 W. Spain St., Sonoma 95476. Telephone: (707) 938-JACK. Hours: 9 a.m.-6 p.m. daily. Cards: BA, MC, AE. Seating: 25 inside, 75 outdoor garden.

DEPOT HOTEL 1870 — *Restaurant*

The Depot Hotel is a gastronomic oasis set on a quiet side street several blocks from Sonoma's historic town square. The outstanding dining experience at the Depot Hotel is complemented by the comfortable and refined ambiance of this landmark structure which was originally built in 1870 and was once owned by General Vallejo. On balmy summer evenings intimate candle-lit tables may be reserved around the outdoor pool.

The "Chef's Choice" menu offers three or four exquisitely prepared entrees each served with hors d'oeuvres, delightful soup du jour, crisp green salad and homemade dessert; the veal and chicken dishes are of particular note.

Depot Hotel 1870, 241 First St. West, Sonoma 95476. Telephone (707) 938-2980. Hours: lunch Fri., Sat., and Mon. 11:30 a.m.-2:00 p.m.; Sunday champagne brunch 10:30 a.m.-2:00 p.m.; Dinner Thurs.-Mon., 5-9 p.m. Price range: lunch $6.00; Brunch $7.50; Dinner $15.00. Corkage: $4.50. Cards: BA, MC, AE. Seating 95. Wine & imported beer.

SONOMA SAUSAGE COMPANY

Now with a new retail outlet "on the square" in Sonoma, the Sonoma Sausage Co. produces some 60 different kinds of sausage. Under the guidance of owner Herb Hoeser, Jr. There is a delicate marjoram coated nurnberger - a variation of bratwurst. The exceptionally sweet weisswurst one made of real, pork, parsley and leaks. The crumbly hausmaker is made only here and in a tiny German town of the same name.

Sonoma Sausage Company, First St. West on the Plaza-411 Sonoma, CA 95476. Telephone: (707) 938-8200. Hours: Summer 9-6 Mon.-Sat., 1-5 Sun Winter 9:30-5:30 Mon.-Sat. 1-5 Sun. Price Range: $1.98-$6.20. No cards accepted.

BOYES HOT SPRINGS

BOYES HOT SPRINGS

BIG THREE FOUNTAIN

Eating at the Big Three is fun. The atmosphere is a cheerful-stark white and forest green, private booths complete with individual Salton toasters, ceiling fans circling overhead, the original 1940's ice cream fountain, cute and efficient waitresses and best of all the food is excellent. (This might be expected considering the meticulous management is the same as the neighboring Sonoma Mission Inn.)

Breakfast at the Big Three centers around substantial three-egg omelettes such as bacon, avocado, tomato and sour cream or ham, potato and scallion. These come served with wheatberry toast, truly outstanding cottage fried potatoes and fresh fruit. The coffee is a rich mocha java blend. The juice is fresh squeezed.

Lunches are equally enjoyable, and might be supplemented with a chilled bottle of local Vino or a splurge on a fountain treat-perhaps a Black & Tan or a fresh Strawberry sundae.

Big Three Fountain, Hwy. 12, Boyes Hot Springs. Telephone: (707) 996-8132. Hours: 8:00 a.m. to 5:00 p.m., seven days a week. Price range: $1.95-$5.75. Seating: 80.

PROVENCAL *Restaurant*

Operating a first class hotel is difficult, managing a first class restaurant even more arduous. To do both successfully is nothing less than a Herculean task. Yet the staff of Sonoma Mission Inn appears to do so with an air of graceful ease.

The restaurant is an awesome, almost monumental structure, an effect enhanced by the stark white, womb-like waiting room. The monochromatic pink interior is vast in proportion, with enormously high beamed ceilings.

A setting such as this generates unusually high expectations for the meal to follow. Happily Provencal lives up to its initial promise.

The extensive menu is a la carte, except on Sunday and Monday nights when a prix fixe limited menu is offered.

On a recent visit this reviewer enjoyed an appetizer of Boudin aux Fruits de Mer, a coarsely ground seafood sausage composed of fresh sole, scallops, shrimp and crab served with a subtly herbed beurre blanc. This was followed by a delightful Caesar salad, crisp romaine lettuce tossed in a classic Caesar dressing garnished with garlic croutons and freshly grated parmesan cheese. Between courses the waiter appeared with tart glasses of sorbet to clear the palate. The exquisite entree of Canard aux Kir Royal, medallions of Petaluma duck breast in an intense brown sauce of champagne and cassis was followed by a dessert of extraordinarily rich chocolate mousse cake and pistachio ice cream. The wine list is extensive and representative of the finest Sonoma County Vintages.

Provencal, 18140 Sonoma Hwy. 12, Boyes Hot Springs, CA 95416. Telephone: (707) 996-1041. Hours: opens daily at 6 p.m. Last dinner seating at 9:30 p.m. Entrees: $13.50-$19.50. Sun.-Mon. (limited menu) $15.50. Sunday brunch 11:30-2:30 p.m., price-$9.95. Seating: 125. Accepted Cards: VISA, MC, AE, & DC.

GLEN ELLEN

SANTA ROSA

THE GLEN ELLEN INN *Restaurant*

Robert Franks and his wife Kei opened their tiny restaurant five years ago in the small town of Glen Ellen.

They have successfully applied their non-commercial approach to food preparation by orienting their customers to the craft of good cooking. They are devotees of the axiom that "the eye eats first". Every carefully prepared dish is not only a pleasure to eat but also a delight to look at.

The menu includes 15 different omelettes, considered by Mr. Franks to be his specialty. The dinner menu offers a choice of 2 entrees which vary daily. Their Sunday brunch is a unique experience in this part of the valley. Specialties include Eggs Benedict, Eggs Florentine and Chicken Liver Omelettes. Another feature of the house is the excellent coffee, the Franks' own blend.

Selected wines from Sonoma and Napa Counties are available.

The moment you enter this well-ordered restaurant you realize the owners pay attention to details. The food is well prepared, the service excellent and the ambiance is tidy and simple.

Glen Ellen Inn, 13670 Arnold Drive, Glen Ellen 95442. Telephone: (707) 938-3478. Hours: Lunch 10:00 a.m.-2:30 p.m.; Dinner 6-9 p.m. Wed.-Sat.; Special Sunday Brunch 10:30a.m.-2:00 p.m. Closed Mon. and Tues. Price range: Lunch $3.00-$5.00; Dinner $7.50-$11.00. No cards. Seating: 28 Reservations recommended.

Travel Notes:

SANTA ROSA

SANTA ROSA

JOHN ASH & COMPANY
Wine Store, Tasting Bar, Restaurant

With the feeling and ambiance of a French Country Inn — John Ash & Company are practioners of what has come to be described as "Creative California Cuisine". With its roots in French cooking, they experiment continually with techniques and flavors from many cuisines. The menu changes continually with prime consideration given to whats fresh and in-season. They go far afield to get unusual ingredients e.g. Opakapaka from Hawaii, Oysters from Louisana, Salmon from Norway.

As an added bonus, the Restaurant combines with a retail wine shop featuring the best of California and European wines. This combination makes for an incredible restaurant wine list as well as a wonderful store in which to browse and sample new releases. A tasting bar provides for the latter. Special emphasis is given to the small "boutique" wineries and many of the wines offered are not available anywhere else in the county.

John Ash & Company, 2324 Montgomery Drive, Santa Rosa, CA 95405. Telephone (707) 527-7687. Hours: Lunch Monday - Friday 11:30 till 2:30. Dinner Wednesday - Sunday 5:30-9°30. Sunday Brunch 10:30-2:00. Wine Store: Open 7 days per week. Cards: VISA, MC.

COURTHOUSE CAFE *Restaurant*

The Courthouse Cafe is a wine drinker's delight. A spacious tasting bar occupies the entry of this comfortable little establishment, where a dozen different-area wines are dispensed by the taste or glass. The black board selection changes daily, offering an opportunity to taste several types and styles of wines in a single visit.

Wine is not the only reason to visit Courthouse Cafe. The food here is attractively presented, imaginatively prepared, and reasonably priced. An interesting pasta dish is always available along with a fresh fish selection (the grilled shark in lemon butter is delightful). The staff is exceedingly friendly and the service efficient.

Courthouse Cafe, 535 - 4th Street, Santa Rosa, CA 95404. Telephone: (707) 523-1171. Hours: Monday - Saturday 11:30 - 2:30. Miday: 2:30 - 6:00. Dinner: Monday thru Thursday - 6:00 - 9:30. Dinner: Friday and Saturday- 6:00 - 10:00. Brunch 10:00 - 3:00. Price Range: Lunch $2.50-$6.00. Dinner: $2.50-$11.50. Cards: MC, VISA. Corkage $3.00. Seating: 95.

CELLAR MASTER WINES *Provisions*

Old railroad square in downtown Santa Rosa provides the historical flavor for this new, innovative wine shop. A thoughtful mixture of oak woodworking and winery photomurals accent a carefully culled selection of premium California and import wines.

A tasting room appropriately appointed in wooden wine crate facings, provides a showcase for the sampling of new wine releases.

Stev Lorenzen, proprietor, draws from his valuable background in the wine trade to direct an operation offering wine evaluation classes, scheduled tastings, books and accessory items, wine storage lockers and, most importantly, expert guidance for both the serious and casual wine imbiber.

Cellar Master Wines, 15 Third St., Santa Rosa. Next to the Marquee Theatre. Telephone (707) 575-1500. Hours: 10 a.m. to 6 p.m. Monday thru Saturday. Closed Sundays. Cards: VISA, MC.

SANTA ROSA

OMELETTE EXPRESS *Restaurant*

The Omelette Express prides itself on having a nearly infinite variety of omelettes; you can concoct your own imaginative creations from their list of over three dozen ingredients. The perfectly cooked omelette comes quickly to your table garnished with fresh fruit, parsley and a thick slab of sourdough bread. If omelettes don't happen to be your thing, lunches include enormous 1/3 pound hamburgers served on French rolls with lettuce, tomatoes, Bermuda onion and potato salad.

Omelette Express, 112 4th Street, Santa Rosa. Telephone (707) 525-1690. Hours: 6:30 a.m.-4:00 p.m. weekdays; 8:00-4:00 Saturday & Sunday. Price range: $2.55-$6.00. Seating: 150.

SANTA ROSA

TRAVERSO'S DELI *Provisions*

Since 1933, the Traverso family has been providing Santa Rosa residents with a fantastic array of gourmet foods, cheese, wine, liquor and Italian cold cuts.

The present building, beautifully constructed, was given a civic award for its architecture and has still retained the image of the "Deli that smells good."

The wine selection is the best in Santa Rosa and includes domestic as well as imported liquors and cordials. Bill Traverso and Steve Lorenzen head the wine department with much knowledge and enthusiasm.

Traverso's, Corner of 3rd and B Sts., Santa Rosa. Telephone (707) 542-2530. Hours: Daily 8:30 a.m.-5:30 p.m. Closed Sundays.

Travel Notes:

SEBASTOPOL

CHEZ PEYO *Restaurant*

Chez Peyo reflects little of its humble origin. The building no longer looks like the exterior of a bowling alley, for it is now covered with an elaborate redwood lattice work. A massive asphalt lot was paved over the old gravel parking area. Inside real linens have replaced the tacky red checkered plastic table cloths. Even the clientele is different. Middle aged upwardly mobile Santa Rosa businessmen discussing the virtues of Jordan wine are sitting at the same tables not long vacated by foodwise alternate lifestyle types. Such is the price of success. One thing at least hasn't changed — the prices.

Chez Peyo still offers one of the best dining values for the dollar anywhere even though the addition of all the ambience amenities seems to have been taken directly out of the food budget. So perhaps the quality is not quite up to the old standards, where else can you get pork loin stuffed with spinach, onion and chicken liver pate baked in puff pastry and topped with Dijon mustard sauce for $7.50? The wine list naturally is Sonoma County oriented.

Chez Peyo, 2795 Gravenstein Hwy. South, Sebastopol 95472. Telephone: (707) 823-1262. Hours: Lunch Tues.-Sat. 11:30-2:30 p.m., Dinner Tues.-Sat. 5:00-10:00 p.m. Sunday 3:00-9:00 p.m. Brunch 10:30-2:00 p.m. Price Range: Lunch $2.99-$6.99 Dinner $5.99-$12.99. Seating: 100. Cards: MC, VISA.

ERNIES LIQUORS *Wine Shop*

Part of the ubiquitous Ernies clan, this Sebastopol outlet is the only wine shop in the area. A substantial selection of Sonoma County wine is featured as well as some Napa, and other areas. Wine glasses, wine books and accessories are also available.

Ernies Liquors, 7140 Keating Ave., Sebastopol 95472. Telephone: (707) 829-0629. Hours: Friday 9:00 a.m.-11:00 p.m., Sunday 9:00 a.m.-8:00 p.m., Mon.-Thurs. & Sat. 9:00 a.m. to 10:00 p.m. Cards: VISA, MC.

LE POMMIER

This French country-style establishment has long been a favorite of Sebastopol residents. It is now co-owned by Chef Tomas Lee & Maitre'd Jess Cenica. The atmosphere remains informal and hospitable. The decor is simple, for the emphasis is on dining.

The dinner menu consists of a well balanced variety of selections, homemade pate, a delicate soup, fresh green salad with cream based vinaigrette, all included in the dinner price. Entrees of fresh fish, poultry, veal, pork, and beef are prepared with classic sauces and presented with fresh vegetables. The Roast Duckling with Gravenstein Apples and Calvados Sauce is worth noting. Le Pommier also serves an interesting luncheon. Salad prepared from local produce and shellfish. Champagne Brunch is served Sundays.

The winelist features twenty varietal wines from Sonoma, Napa and Mendocino counties.

Le Pommier, 1015 Gravenstein Hwy. So., Sebastopol 95472. Telephone: (707) 823-9865. Hours: Dinner 5:00-9:00 p.m. Tues.-Sun; Lunch 11:30-3:00 p.m. Tues.-Fri.; Sunday Brunch 11:00 a.m.-2:30 p.m. Price range: Dinner $7.50-$12.00; Lunch $4.00-$6.00. Corkage: $3.50. Cards: VISA, MC. Seating: 82.

FORESTVILLE

GUERNEVILLE

CASA DE JOANNA *Restaurant*
Diners work up quite an appetite simply trying to find Casa De Joanna. But once they've found it-an appetite will come in handy.

Portions on the menu are truly immense but, surprisingly the quantity comes in a close second to the quality.

All food is prepared fresh to order. No frozen or prepackaged products taint the meal. Recipes are a personalized interpretation of Mexican cuisine such as the Enchillada de Res, positively stuffed with shredded beef, chopped olives, and red onions, covered with red chile sauce and melted cheddar, then topped with sour cream. The Taquitos are corn tortillas rolled into flutes, filled with shredded beef, then deep fried, topped with guacamole, sour cream, and diced tomatoes.

Casa De Joanna, off Neely at Orchard and River Guerneville, CA 95446. Telephone: (707) 869-3756. Price range: $6.25-$10.50. Seating: 75. Cards: MC VISA. Hours: closed Tuesday and Wednesday, open Thursday thru Monday 5:00-9:00.

L'OMELETTE *Restaurant*
Leon Arseguel began his gourmet cooking career when he was a boy and has been preparing French meals for fifty-two years. After retiring once, he and his wife, Antoinette, opened this intimate cafe in the center of Forestville.

Complete dinners including soup, salad, potato, vegetable and coffee, are very reasonably priced. Specialty entrees include Breast of Capon Monte Carlo, Tournedos Filet of Beef, and Coquille of Sea Food Riviera, a combination of shrimp, scallops and mushrooms in cream sauce.

L'Omelette, 6685 Front St., Forestville 95436. Telephone: (707) 887-9945. Hours: 5:30-9:00p.m. Fri.-Sun. only. Price range: $6.50-$11.50. No cards, no checks. Seating: 30.

FRANCES' SEA FOOD MARKET *Market*
On your way to the beach? Expecting to pick up fresh fish at the local market? Forget it. There isn't any to be found once you're there. Stop instead at Frances' Sea Food Market on your way to or from the coast. Absolutely the freshest sea food available; Salmon, shrimp, Squid, you name it.

As Frances' business card says, "We specialize in ocean-fresh fish from our own boats." Believe it.

Frances' Sea Food Market, Safeway parking lot, Guerneville, CA. Telephone: (707) 869-0701. Hours: 10:00-6:00 every day. No cards.

BODEGA BAY

DUNCAN'S MILLS

BODEGA GALLERY *Restaurant*

Near the coastal village of Bodega Bay is the Bodega Gallery and Restaurant. Yes, this is the original Bodega school house built in 1873, and made famous in the 1963 Hitchcock film "The Birds". Indeed daily menus are written on the school blackboard. This intimate little cafe specializes in soups, salads, quiche, crepes and a seafood catch of the day. Meals are prepared using fresh ingredients in a reassuring style. Owners Mary Leah Taylor and her father, are friendly and go out of their way to accommodate guests. The wine list is limited to selections from three Sonoma Wineries.

Bodega Gallery Restaurant, 1710 Bodega Ln. Bodega, CA 94922. Telephone: (707) 876-3257. Price range: Dinner, $6.95-$13.55. Hours: Thursday-Friday; Lunch 12:00-2:30 p.m., Dinner 5:00-9:00 p.m. Saturday 12:00 10:00 p.m. Sunday, Brunch 10:00 a.m.-2:00 p.m., Dinner-2:00 p.m.-8:00 p.m. Closed one month during Christmas season. Seating 38. Cards: MC, VISA. Reservations advised.

THE BLUE HERON *Restaurant*

Duncan's Mills has been around since the Russian River's logging days. The Mills are gone but the village remains relatively intact, unspoiled by the up-river summer home developments.

Resting on a slope above the river bank is the Blue Heron. The restaurant is entered through the bar where tourists and a colorful mix of locals have a chance to mingle before eating. The dining room has a woodsy sort of feel with the work of craftsman evident in much redwood detailing. Picture windows line the walls, providing a lovely view of the undulating hillsides.

Don't be discouraged by the fact that the kitchen specializes in "vegetarian cuisine". There are always enticing entrees featuring fresh fish and imaginatively prepared chicken dishes. Meals are served with hearty soups, fresh greens, and homemade bread. The wine list emphasizes Sonoma County wines.

Blue Heron, Duncan's Mills, Ca. Telephone (707) 865-2269. Hours: Lunch 12:00-4:00 daily. Dinner 5:30-9:30 daily. Monday night entertainment. Thursday Community night. Closed Monday, Tuesday and Wednesday in Winter. Sunday 10:00-2:00 Brunch. Price Range: Lunch $2.50-$5.75. Dinner $5.00-$10.00.

HEALDSBURG

COSTEAUX FRENCH BAKERY

The red and white striped awning hanging in front marks this bakery a block and a half north of the Plaza in downtown Healdsburg.

Karl Seppi, a real estate broker turned baker, and his wife, Nancy, create a Sourdough French bread perfect for picnics on the Russian River.

Their efforts also include a tasty assortment of French pastries.

Costeaux French Bakery, 421 Healdsburg Ave, Healdsburg. Telephone: (707) 433-1913. Hours: Wed.-Sat. 7:00 a.m.-5:00 p.m. Sun. 7:00-12:30 p.m. Closed Mon. and Tues. No cards.

GEYSERVILLE

WINE COUNTRY RESTAURANT   *Restaurant*

What looks like an old concrete wine warehouse on the town square is in actuality Healdsburg's most popular restaurant. Inside it still looks like a winery, but the crisp white linens, bentwood chairs, private booths help to warm things up. The staff is friendly and the prices reasonable. The food is fresh and simply prepared in a provencial style. The wine list features Sonoma wines by the glass and by the bottle.

Wine Country Restaurant, 106 Matheson, Healdsburg, CA. Telephone (707) 433-7203. Hours: Lunch 11:00-2:00. Dinner: 5:30-9:30 seven days a week. Live entertainment Wednesday-Sunday evenings. Price range: Lunch $4.25 average. Dinner $6.25-$15.00. Cards: Visa, Master Charge, American Express. Corkage $3.00.

SOUVERAIN   *Restaurant/Winery*

It would be grossly inappropriate to exclude from a wine touring publication the only restaurant actually located at a winery in the area. And the restaurant at Souverain is exciting, not only because it resides in such a dramatic architectural setting but commands one of the finest views in all of Alexander Valley.

While dining on the scenic terrace, the vine clad Alexander Valley lies to the foreground of Mt. St. Helena looming on the horizon.

The food is French and the wine is Souverain. There are daily special entrees, often fresh fish, and all wines are sold at tasting room prices.

Souverain, 400 Souverain Road, Geyserville. (take Independence Lane exit off Hwy. 101.) Telephone: (707) 433-3141. Hours: Lunch 11-3 p.m. Mon.-Sat.; Dinner 5-9 p.m. Wed.-Sun.; Champagne Brunch 10:30-2:30 p.m. Sun. Price range: Lunch $5.50-$8.50; Dinner $9.00-$18.00. Cards: VISA, MC. Reservations recommended. Call for winter hours.

UKIAH

REDWOOD VALLEY/UKIAH

CHICK'S HOUSE OF SPIRITS *Provisions*

The wine selection here is more comprehensive than any other store in Ukiah. With over 300 selections of wine, the large underground cellar consists of well-displayed bottles from several of the larger Sonoma and Napa wineries, most of the local Mendocino wineries, and quite a number of imports. Several shelves of wine books are available for reference and for sale.

Upstairs amid the liquor, pop wine, and party supplies, is a small counter of delicatessen cheeses, meats, salads and gourmet sandwiches all moderately priced.

Chick's House of Spirits, 290 So. State St., Ukiah 95482. Telephone: (707) 462-5663. Hours: 10 a.m. - 10 p.m. Monday-Thursday; 10 a.m.-12 p.m. Fridays and Saturdays; 10 a.m.-8 p.m. Sunday. Cards: BA, MC.

BROILER STEAK HOUSE *Restaurant, Bar*

As the name suggests the specialty of the house is pit-broiled steak, cooked the "old California way" over oak wood. Among the favorites are the Special Dinner Steak ($7.50), an incredibly tender Broiled Filet Steak ($11.00), and Surf and Turf ($15.75); but a variety of juicy steaks cooked to your taste are available on the menu in addition to barbequed spareribs and chicken and several seafood choices.

Broiler Steak House, Uva Drive, Redwood Valley 95470. Telephone: (707) 485-7301. Hours: 4-11 p.m. Monday-Saturday, 3-10 p.m. Sunday. Price range: $3.25-$15.75. Cards: BA, MC. Seating: 600. Full bar service and cocktail lounge.

HENNE'S ICE CREAM *Provisions*

The Henne family maintains the old-fashioned high quality by using fresh cream and other natural ingredients in their ice cream and candies, all of which they produce right there in the shop. Any one of the eighteen to twenty flavors of ice cream exudes freshness and richness.

Real ice cream enthusiasts will rejoice when they see the prices here. Hand-packed pints go for $1.25 and quarts for $2.40.

Henne's Homemade Candies & Ice Cream, 582 No. State St., Ukiah 95482. Telephone (707) 462-5661. Hours: Fall to Spring, Sunday-Wednesday 12:30-9:00 p.m., Thursday-Saturday 12:30-10:00 p.m.; Summer 12:00 a.m.-10:00 p.m. daily. Cards: BA, MC.

GUALALA

ST. ORRES — *Restaurant, Inn*

St. Orres is the indisputable dining choice in the Gualala area of the coast. After all, this is really the only quality restaurant around and even if you're not nearby, it's worth the drive just to look at the architecture. The building and interior were entirely handcrafted by the owners and local artisans. The place resembles nothing more than a miniature Russian palace, with handcarved redwood onion-top turrets and stained glass windows. Through the cozy parlor with its hobbit-style stone fireplace, double oak doors lead to the spectacular dining room with its domed turret rising fifty feet. Light filters down through three stories of paned windows affording dramatic views of forest and sea. Deep carpeting, fresh flowers and local stoneware help set the scene.

The four owners of St. Orres all work on the premises and take part in the constantly changing menu selection where there is always a bit of experimentation. The cuisine is French and the menu, imaginative, and there is always fresh fish available. The salmon when in season is a must.

St. Orres is also an inn with 8 small handcrafted rooms, two overlooking the sea, and 3 cottages with kitchens and private baths, and fireplaces.

St. Orres, P.O. Box 523, Gualala 95445. Telephone: (707) 884-3303. Rates: $45.00-$90.00 including continental breakfast. Restaurant hours: Dinner 6-9 p.m. Sun.-Fri., 5:30-9:30 Sat.; Brunch 11:30-2:30 Sun. only. Price range: Brunch $5.75; Dinner $10.00-$18.00. Cards: VISA, MC for room only. Number of rooms: 8. Number of cottages: 3.

BOONVILLE

BOONVILLE HOTEL — *Restaurant*

Managing partners Vernon and Charlene Rollins have a special vision of gourmet environment, a kind of sleek 30's modern which goes with their unique menu. Home simplicity and elegance are the keynotes to dining at the Boonville Hotel. The Rollns' grow or assemble all ingredients locally including homemade pasta, garden vegetables, ranch meat, fresh mussels or squid. The menu is entirely al la carte, create your own meal from the appetizers main courses, side dishes, salads and desserts of the day. The wine list is mostly Anderson Valley and excellent.

The restaurant is open daily all year for meals, snacks, and coffee from 11:30 a.m. There is a full bar where you can mingle with tired drummers, boisterous loggers, cattlemen and assorted locals.

Boonville Hotel, 14040 Hwy. 128, Boonville, CA (707) 895-3478. Hours: 11:30-10:00 7 days a week. Price Range: $3.95-$12.50. Credit Cards: None.

LITTLE RIVER   MENDOCINO

LITTLE RIVER CAFE *Restaurant*

The Little River Cafe is not the kind of place that you just impulsively drop in. First of all, you won't be able to find it unless you know where to look. It is hidden away in the back of the local post office and directly across the highway from Little River Inn.

The view of the adjacent coast is marvelous; unfortunately only the chef can enjoy it because the kitchen occupies the view side of the restaurant. Patrons are squeezed into the seven tables of this tiny, but ever so attractive, little establishment.

So why bother, the reader might ask. For one reason only - the Little River Cafe is probably the best restaurant on the North Coast. It is owned and operated by Nancy Alford and Robert Rutley. Nancy presides over the kitchen with grace and expertise. Her food is fresh, the cuisine creative and the presentation artful. There are two seatings nightly; each begins as guests are greeted by gracious host Robert Rutley. A warm freshly-baked loaf is carried steaming from the oven and distributed to the tables. The soup, always impressive, was on a recent visit, a subtle carrot puree, delicately spiced with thyme. The entrees which vary nightly are classic in origin but bear the chef's innovative stamp. On the same occasion, entrees were fresh albacore with a delightfully green cucumber cream sauce, and boned breast of chicken sauteed with local apples, gruyere cheese and shallot sauce. Each was served with snow peas, carrots, mushrooms, and peeled cherry tomatoes, all lightly sauteed in butter and sprinkled with parmesan cheese. The wine list is quite eclectic and reflects the owners' highly individual tastes.

Little River Cafe, Little River, CA 95456. Telephone: (707) 937-0404. Hours: Friday-Monday seatings at 6:30 p.m. and 8:30 p.m. Price range: approx. $15.00. Seating: 18. Cards: no cards. Reservations taken for locals, repeat customers and parties of five or more.

CAFE BEAUJOLAIS *Restaurant*

Set in the relaxed country atmosphere of one of Mendocino's older homes, owner Margaret Fox's hospitality reaches out of the pastel-printed wallpaper to the antique oak tables, every one complete with fresh cut flowers. There is a big deck in back which overlooks Big River and the ocean, perfect for luncheon.

Friday through Sunday's dinner is Table d'hote, complete with homemade bread, sweet butter, soup of the day, salad, rice or potatoes, vegetable and coffee. The entree is cooked French style and varies depending upon local fresh food availabilities.

Breakfasts include a choice of omelettes, waffles, fruit and coffee cakes. Lunches offer omelettes, quiche, soup, fruit salad and sandwiches. The conspicuous freshness of all items is highlighted by the fact that nearly everything is homemade or homegrown.

A most interesting wine list includes varieties from Sonoma, Mendocino and Napa, and a good selection of French and German wines.

Cafe Beaujolais, 961 East Ukiah St., Mendocino 95460. Telephone (707) 937-5614. Hours: Breakfast 7:30 a.m.-2 p.m. (9 a.m.-2 p.m. Sundays) Daily; Lunch 11:30 a.m.-2 p.m. Daily; Dinner 6-9 p.m. Fri.-Mon. (during the spring and summer.) Price range: Breakfast $1.00-$6.00; Lunch $2.50-$6.50; Dinner $8.00-$12.00. Corkage $2.50. Reservations recommended. Seating 40 plus 20 on the patio.

THE SEAGULL — *Restaurant*

After recovering from a disastrous fire in December, 1976, which burned their business to the ground, owners David and Cathy Jones have recently opened the new Seagull. The modern angular architecture distinguishes the structure markedly from the standard New England style which predominates in Mendocino. The use of natural wood grain, house plants, and contemporary stained glass windows provides a relaxed atmosphere in this extravagant coffee shop.

Undeniably the favorite breakfast spot in town, the Seagull offers a complete menu of juices, fruits, eggs, omelettes, and other familiar favorites. Lunches feature a variety of sandwiches and salads.

The dinner menu is surprisingly varied, specializing in seafood. The Bouillabaise on the a la carte section is a rich stock of fresh fish, shrimp and clams. Also on the a la carte section is a bargain soup and salad dinner with French bread and wine for $5.95. The wine list features a few small Mendocino County labels along with other more standard California wineries.

One of the big attractions to the Seagull is the "Cellarbar" located upstairs from the restaurant. Here comfortable chairs around a large fire pit and before a wall of plate glass windows offer a leisurely setting.

The Seagull, cnr. Lansing and Ukiah Sts., Mendocino 95460. Telephone: (707) 937-5204. Hours: 8:00 a.m.-9:00 p.m. Price range: Breakfast, $1.55-$6.75; Lunch $1.95-$6.75; Dinner $4.95-$11.50. Weekday luncheon specials $3.50. No cards. Full bar. Seating: 55.

Travel Notes: _____
_____
_____
_____

THE CHEESE SHOP — *Provisions*

The Cheese Shop is owned and operated by Rob Ferrero. The shop showcases an extensive offering of imported and domestic cheese and gourmet food specialties including pates, baguettes, croissants, mustards and homemade jellies and jams. The list goes on.

The "Wine Cellar" holds mostly premium California wines with an obvious emphasis on Mendocino labels. The Wine Bar is open weekends providing an opportunity to taste and enjoy several wines simultaneously. The remainder of the shop is devoted to gift ware. Among the eyecatchers are imported baskets, linens, glassware and gourmet cooking utensils.

The Cheese Shop, Corner Little Lake and Lansing Sts. Mendocino 95460. Telephone: (707) 937-0104 Hours: Winter 10:30-5:30 p.m. Closed Wed. Sunday 10:30-3:00 p.m. Summer 10-6 everyday Sunday 10-4 p.m.

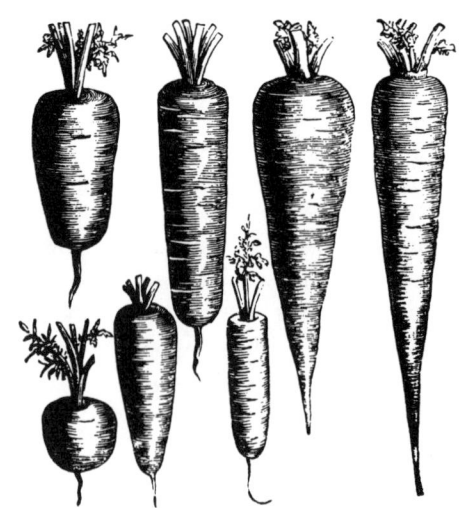

The editors have had numerous requests to provide a qualitative listing of Sonoma and Mendocino County restaurants. While it should be remembered that restaurants selected for review in the Sonoma and Mendocino County Wine Tour appear here only because they are in some way noteworthy, we have decided to further qualify restaurants by selecting-through a polling system—the "Ten Best Sonoma and Mendocino County Restaurants." These have been selected by a representative group of Sonoma and Mendocino County Vintners as being their "favorite" restaurants.

We have tried to provide not only a broad geographical distribution but have singled out which meals are the most favored in each particular restaurant. The top ten restaurants are represented in this section by reproductions of their menus.

PLEASE NOTE:

Menus and prices will change. Some restaurants included in this section have a policy of changing their menus daily or weekly. These menus are included only to give an indication of menu and price range.

CAFE BEAUJOLAIS
916 Ukiah St., Mendocino, CA 95460 (707) 937-5614

CAFE BEAUJOLAIS

Breakfast 7:30 to 2   Lunch 11:30 to 2   Sunday Brunch 9 to 2

Egg Dishes

served with your choice of toast, coffee cake, english muffins, bagel or homemade muffins with croissant, add .50

Special Omelette of the day	4.75
Linguisa Omelette	4.75
Herb Omelette *(prepared with Fuller's Fine Herbs)*	3.50
Cheese Omelette	3.85
Mushroom & Sour Cream Omelette	4.25
Green Chile & Cheese Omelette	4.25
Herbed Cream Cheese Omelette	4.25
Bacon & 3 Scrambled Eggs	3.85
Country Sausage & 3 Scrambled Eggs	3.95

for each additional ingredient 75

A la Carte

Waffles *tangy, made with buttermilk, cornmeal and oatmeal, served with real maple syrup* 2.40
with fruit or yogurt 3.40   *with fruit and yogurt* 3.95

French Toast *served with real maple syrup* 3.00
with fruit or yogurt 4.00   *with fruit and yogurt* 4.50

Suzanne's Famous Cashew Granola *with fresh fruit* 1.75

Hot Cereal 1.35   *with raisins* 1.65

Fresh Fruit Salad *(in season)* small 1.75   large 3.25   *with yogurt or cottage cheese* 4.00
with creme fraiche 4.25

Side Orders

Scrambled or Fried Eggs   *one* .85   *two* 1.30   *three* 1.65

Bacon 1.45   Country Sausage 1.80   Ham 1.80   Country Fries 1.25   Coffee Cake 1.25

Toast .75   Bran Muffins .85   English Muffins, Bagels .85   Croissant 1.25

Cream Cheese .75   Yogurt .95   Sour Cream .95   Creme Fraiche 1.00

Cottage Cheese .95

THE BLUE HERON INN
Hwy. 116, Duncans Mills, CA (707)865-2269

The Blue Heron Inn
Duncans Mills

2/28

Special Dinners of the Evening

International Vegetarian Specialties

7.00 Spinach-Mushroom Lasagne — Sautéed spinach, mushrooms and onions with layers of ricotta, mozzarella and provolone cheese with spinach noodles. Topped with a rich tomato-wine sauce. Served with vegetables.

6.00 Tofu Teriyaki — Tofu marinated and broiled in a sauce of tamari, white miso, fresh ginger and garlic. Served with rice and steamed vegetables.

South of the Border

7.50 Vegetable Cheese Enchiladas — Two tender corn tortillas filled with sautéed fresh mushrooms, zucchini, scallions, jalapeño peppers and Jack cheese. Topped with Salsa Roja, served with refried beans, sour cream and Salsa Fresca.

Chicken (Please allow ½ hour to prepare)

10.50 Brandied Chicken — Two tender breasts of chicken browned lightly in butter, then sautéed with white wine and brandy, finished with cream.

Fish

8.50 Fresh Filet of Pacific Red Snapper with a choice of preparations:
A. Sautéed in garlic butter with white wine and mushrooms
OR
B. Veracruzana — marinated then broiled and topped with Salsa Fresca.

PROVENCAL
18140 Sonoma Hwy. 12, Boyes Hot Springs, CA 95416 (707) 996-1041

Hors-d'Oeuvre Froids

Paté de Canard
Homemade duck paté perfumed with port and brandy with pistachio nuts.
5.00

Saumon and Esturgeon Fumé
Smoked Bodega Bay salmon and Oregon sturgeon with classic garnish.
6.50

Écrevisse au Cognac
Fresh Sacramento crayfish and artichokes tossed in a cognac flavored mayonnaise.
7.50

Caviar American
Fresh golden caviar served in the classic style.
7.50

Les Salades

Salade César
Crisp Romaine lettuce tossed in a classic Caesar dressing, garnished with garlic croutons and freshly grated parmesan cheese.
4.00

Salade Exotique
Aged Smithfield ham tossed with fresh fruits in a champagne dressing.
7.50

La Salade Provençale
A salad of sliced fresh tomatoes, avocados garnished with enok mushrooms served with a sesame seed oil vinaigrette dressing.
4.50

Salade Panachée
A mixed country salad with the dressing of your choice.
3.00

Les Poissons

Coquilles Saint Jacques en Surprise
Fresh eastern scallops with herb butter under a golden pastry.
14.50

Poisson à la Façon des Cuisiniers
A daily fish creation from the kitchen.
(Depends on the catch)

Escalope of Saumon Oriental
Fresh Bodega Bay salmon thinly sliced and served with a ginger and scallion butter sauce.
14.00

Hors-d'Oeuvre Chauds

Potage du jour
3.00

Pasta Primavera
Homemade green and white fettucini, garden fresh vegetables, tossed in cream, basil, pine nuts and a touch of garlic.
4.50

Boudin aux Fruits de Mer
A seafood sausage of fresh sole, scallops, shrimp and crab served with a butter fondue seasoned with fine herbs and garnished with a julienne of cucumber.
5.50

Les Entrées

Suprême de Volaille du Chef
The Chef's daily chicken creation.
10.50

Canard au Kir Royal
Fresh Petaluma duckling boned and sliced and served with a champagne and cassis sauce.
14.50

Côte de Veau farcie
A tender veal chop filled with a mushroom purée, liver paté, sautéed accompanied with glazed baby onions, served with a creamy shallot sauce.
15.50

Selle d'Agneau Feuilletée
A boneless saddle of lamb smothered with a mushroom purée, baked in puff pastry until golden brown, served with creamy green peppercorn sauce.
16.50

Salade de Volaille Froid
Chicken breasts marinated in teriyaki, served cold with fresh vegetables with Russian dressing.
12.50

Les Grillades et les Rôtis

Filet de Boeuf Grillé
A filet of beef grilled to your taste, accompanied with bearnaise and a Madeira mushroom sauce.
16.50

Carré d'Agneau Rôti au Persil
Rack of lamb coated with bread crumbs, parsley and a hint of garlic, roasted to your taste, served in its natural juices.
16.50

Squab
Fresh Petaluma squab, grilled and served with a mustard and herb butter sauce.
13.50

Poisson du jour Grillé
Grilled fresh fish of the day.
(Depends on the catch)

CAFE PILOU
Place des Pyrenees-464 First St. East, Sonoma, CA 95476 (707)996-2157

CAFÉ Pilou

OMELETTES
#1 Jack, Swiss or Cheddar   3.50
#2 Mushrooms, Green Onions, Herbs & Cheese   3.75
#3 Fresh Spinach, Tomatoes & Sour Cream   4.25
#4 Basque Piperade   4.50
#5 Ham, Cheese & Ranchero Sauce   4.25

TWO BAKED, SCRAMBLED OR FRIED EGGS   2.50
with Ranchero Sauce & Cheese   3.25
with Piperade   3.75
with Sausage   3.75
We use fertile eggs, cream & fresh vegetables.

FRENCH TOAST MAISON   3.50
Sonoma French Bread soaked in eggs, cream and spices

FRESH FRUIT BOWL   2.75
Freshly Cut Seasonal Fruits
with Yogurt or sour cream . . . add   .80

APPETIZERS
Soup du Jour
French Onion Soup Gratinée   2.25
Appetizer Salad   3.95
selections from four prepared or marinated salads
Small Appetizer Salad, a selection of one or two   2.25
Pâté Maison et Salade Verte, Cornichons   4.00
Piperade Basquaise   2.75

SALADES
House Dressing or Vinaigrette
Tossed Butter Lettuce   2.25
Albacore on lettuce, tomatoes, peppers, olives, cornichons   4.75
Bay Shrimp on lettuce, tomatoes, peppers, olives, cornichons   5.75
Spinach Salade, mushrooms, sweet onions,
chopped eggs, olives and tomatoes   3.95

ENTREES
Served from 11:00 A.M.
Sonoma French Bakery Bread & Sweet Butter accompany all meals.

PLAT du JOUR * see blackboard

TORTE d'EPINARDS, SALADE VERTE   5.75
a spinach torte made with eggs, basil, ricotta and cheddar cheeses

ASSIÈTTE CHARCUTIÈRE   5.95
cold assortment of meats and stuffed pork loin
French potato salade

PILOU PLATTER   5.95
Half cold roasted chicken with French potato salade or Pommes Frites

TORTE d'OGNIONS with SALADE VERTE   5.25

LE HAMBURGER   4.25
on Sonoma French Bread with lettuce, tomatoes, onions,
Pilou mayonnaise & Pommes Frites
(with Jack, Swiss or Cheddar Cheese . . . add .50)

BIG THREE FOUNTAIN
Sonoma Hwy. 12, Boyes Hot Springs, CA 95416 (707) 996-8132

Lunch
11 to 3 Daily

Sandwiches

All sandwiches served with fresh garden salad, fresh fruit or cottage fried potatoes

Avocado, Bacon & Tomato	3.95
Bacon, Lettuce & Tomato	3.50
Avocado, Cream Cheese & Tomato	3.50
Ham & Cheese Sandwich	4.25
White Meat Tuna Water packed	4.25
Fresh Baked Chicken & Cheese	3.95
Shrimp Salad Sandwich	4.35
Steak Sandwich	6.95
Hamburger With cheese - add .50	3.75

Salads

All salads served with sourdough French bread & butter

Shrimp Salad	5.50
Fresh Fruit & Cottage Cheese	4.35
Garden Salad	3.75
Spinach Salad	4.35
Chef's Salad	5.20
Chicken Salad	4.50
Small Green Salad	1.95

Additions and Substitutions extra

LITTLE RIVER CAFE

each entree includes fresh bread, soup and salad

fresh salmon poached - court bouillion with raspberry salad sauce

fillets of sirloin tip stuffed with pinenuts, cheeses and italian ham. rolled, braised and simmered in red wine tomatoe sauce.

roast duckling with honey and soy glaze and pomegranate sauce

$15.00

ST. ORRES

Hwy. 1, Gualala, CA 95445 (707) 884-3335

Entrées

Poisson du Jour

Prawns Bordelaise — 13.50
Prawns sautéed with garlic, shallots, white wine, butter and parsley.

Cari de Suprême de Volaille — 12.50
Chicken breast sautéed with curry, onions, apples and cream and served with mango chutney, almonds and raisins.

Sauté de Veau Aux Champignons — 14.00
Veal tenderloin sautéed with mushrooms, cream, madeira and demi-glace.

Canard Aux Papayer — 12.75
Roast duckling with fresh papayas, oranges and sauce Bigarade.

Entrecôte Au Poivre Vert — 14.50
New York steak sautéed and served with a sauce of green peppercorns, brandy and cream.

Filet de Boeuf Bearnaise — 15.25
Beef tenderloin sautéed and served with sauce Bearnaise.

Carré D'Agneau Dijonnaise — 16.75
Roast rack of lamb in a crust of Dijon mustard, garlic, parsley and breadcrumbs.

EASTSIDE GRILL
133 East Napa St., Sonoma, CA 95476 (707) 938-4909

THE EASTSIDE GRILL

Open
11 a.m. - 11 p.m.
Closed
Wednesday

133 East Napa St.
Sonoma
California
938-4909

SEAFOOD APPETIZERS

Fresh Shucked
on the Half Shell
½ doz. oysters   4.00
½ doz. clams   4.00

Cocktails
Crab   3.75
Shrimp   3.50
Bay Scallops 3.50

PASTA

Pasta Pesto alla Filipello
Tagliarini   6.00
Tortellini   6.00
Seafood Pasta   9.50
Canneloni   6.50

SALADS

Green Dinner   1.75
Seafood   7.75
Fresh Fruit   5.75

ENTREES

From the Mexican Mesquite Charcoal Grill
served with Rice and Vegetable
See chalkboard for availability and price

FRESH SEAFOOD

Live
Maine Lobster

Red Snapper
Salmon
Sea Bass
Ling Cod

Seafood Brochette

Surf & Turf

Halibut
Tuna
Shad Roe
Swordfish
Shark

POULTRY & MEATS

Rabbit
Game Bird

New York Steak
Pork Chops
Lamb

DESSERTS

Homemade
Ice Cream

Cheese & Fruits
Fresh Berries with Whipped Cream

Pastries

JOHN ASH & COMPANY
2324 Montgomery Dr., Santa Rosa, CA 95405 (707) 527-7687

John Ash & Company

Pastas

(our own fresh made pasta served with french bread and sweet butter)

Green Tortellini .... $4.25 whole
"Little hats" filled with veal, mortadella in a sauce $2.75 half
of cream, fontina and asiago cheeses

Linguini With Pesto .... $3.95 whole
Thin linguini egg and spinach noodles in a sauce of $2.50 half
fresh basil, garlic and parmesan cheese

Fettucine "Alfredo" .... $3.95 whole
Our version of the classic with cream, sweet butter, $2.50 half
imported cheeses and proscuitto

Egg Dishes

(served with sour French bread and sweet butter)

Omelette Paysanne $3.95
A flat omelette with new potatoes, smoked ham,
onions and herbs

Omelette Piperade $3.95
A folded omelette with sweet peppers,
onions and mushrooms

Special Sandwiches

(served with vegetables vinaigrette)

Italiene $4.25
Proscuitto, sweet onions, fontina and gruyere cheeses
on special fogaccia bread

Manhattan $4.50
Smoked Salmon, natural cream cheese on a fresh bagel

Apple Jack $2.95
Sliced tart apples, Sonoma Jack and Swiss Gruyere cheeses
with a mild curry mayonnaise on whole grain bread

Ash & Company Special Hamburgers (on whole grain or sour french)
— with sweet peppers, onions and mushrooms $3.95
— with green chilis and Sonoma Jack cheese $3.95
— plain and simple $3.75

Soups

French Onion Gratinee $2.50
The classic long-simmered version topped with a croute
and imported Gruyere and parmesan cheeses

COURTHOUSE CAFE

535 Fourth St., Santa Rosa, CA 95404
(707) 523-1171

DINNER

APPETIZERS

Marinated Herring   2.95
In wine and herbs with red onion, sour cream and flat bread.

Chicken Liver Mousse   1.95
*A mousse of chicken livers, port wine, herbs,
garlic and butter.*

Country Style Paté   3.50   (half order   1.95)
With cornichons, mustard and sour French bread.

Fresh Marinated Vegetables   3.25   (half order   1.75)
Seasonal raw vegetables in a lemon marinade.

Courthouse Cafe Escargot   3.50
Fresh herb garlic butter, chopped walnuts, pimiento and Asiago cheese.

DAILY SPECIALS

Every day we seek out the freshest
available ingredients to prepare special dishes. Please
ask your waitperson about today's offerings.

ENTREES

*entrees are served with seasonal fresh vegetables,
French bread and sweet butter.*

Quiche of the Day   5.25
*Fresh eggs, cream, imported gruyere cheese and herbs,
with changing daily additions in a pastry crust.*

Fettuccine Bianco   5.95
*A variation of the classic "Alfredo," with Asiago cheese, eggs,
cream, sweet peas and pepper.*

Pasta Marco Polo   5.95
*Ms. Child's recipe with walnuts, black olives, basil, Parmesan
and Asiago cheeses, pimiento and garlic tossed quickly with linguini noodles.*

"Smothered" Chicken   6.50
*An old southern recipe of fresh chicken simmered
in a flavorful stock with mushrooms, herbs, onions and cream.*

Fresh Catch of the Day
A special preparation of the best fresh fish we can find.

Red Snapper "en papillote"   7.25
*Fresh snapper baked in parchment with a light white wine sauce,
bay shrimp, lemon and herbs.*

Lobster "St. Denis"   7.95
*Half a Baja lobster served cold with a Russian specialty
of potatoes, eggs, beets and sour cream.*

Grilled Lamb Chops   8.50
*Baby lamb chops, marinated in lemon and herbs
and quickly grilled.*

Petite Filet Dijonnaise   9.50
*Aged beef filet, pan broiled and finished with a deglaze of wine,
cream, mushrooms and Dijon mustard.*

SONOMA

Travelers to the regions north of San Francisco Bay have a variety of sights, sounds and smells from which to choose. Viewing the natural beauty of California's mountain ridges pitching to the sea is one of man's favorite pastimes. The coast line stretching along Sonoma and Mendocino Counties is magnificent, whether fog-shrouded or crystal clear. The orchards, meadows and fields of the agricultural region of Sonoma County convey a peaceful reassurance in contrast to the urban centers only a few hours away, while the unspoiled splendor of Mendocino's towering redwood forests remain seemingly invulnerable.

Such appealing attributes have long enchanted visitors to both counties although to complete the picture, visits to the local wineries are essential. There is a mystical, timeless quality in the experience of inhaling the aroma that lingers in the cellars, in viewing the casks and barrels that contain so much wine, and in sampling the product where it is made. After a full day of touring winery facilities and tasting rooms, the visitor may have need of rest.

The following hotels, inns, resorts, and campgrounds have been listed to aid the overnight visitor to the wine country of Sonoma and Mendocino. The variety offered is extensive due largely to the broad area covered, although there are numerous other campgrounds along the Russian River and the coast and scattered among the redwoods in Mendocino County.

Reservations for desired accommodations are advisable during the peak touring months from May to November.

Travel Notes:_____
_____
_____
_____

CHALET BED & BREAKFAST *Inn*

The Swiss gentleman who built this quaint little chalet adorned the walls with murals of his beloved homeland. The rooms are cluttered with antiques and lacework; peacocks stroll through the lush garden. All within a short walking distance of town, visitors are transported both in time and space to a cozy turn-of-the-century Swiss farm house. The four guest rooms share two baths. Upstairs a sitting room is warmed by a pot-bellied stove. A real country breakfast is served, with ranch eggs, fresh fruit and muffins. A hot tub is available for private bathing.

Chalet Bed & Breakfast, 18935-5th street, West Sonoma, CA 95475. Telephone: (707) 996-0190. Rates: $45.00-$55.00. Number of rooms: 4. No cards.

SONOMA HOTEL *Lodging*

The Sonoma Hotel will take the traveler back through its 100 years of history and acquaint him with the charm of an old world caravansary.

This three-story hotel, located at Spain Street and First Street West, has been recently renovated by owners John and Dorene Musilli. Old time bathtubs in five rooms, lovely old beds, antiques from Europe and California heirlooms are found in each of the seventeen beautiful rooms. An interesting brochure from the Sonoma Hotel lists all of the room accommodations, furnishings and locations for advance planners.

Sonoma Hotel, corner Spain Street & First Street West, Sonoma 95476. Telephone (707) 996-2996. Rates: $35.00-$55.00 (doubles) with Continental breakfast.

BOYES HOT SPRINGS

SONOMA MISSION INN *Inn*

The Sonoma Mission Inn was originally constructed in 1926. For nearly two decades it reigned as Sonoma County's most fashionable resort. After World War II, a period of neglect set in. In 1980 Ed Safdie purchased the aging landmark and under his direction it has been dramatically transferred into a first class luxury hotel.

A fifty foot water tower emblazoned with the Sonoma Mission Inn monogram marks the Inn's location west of Hwy. 12. A circular tree-lined drive leads to the three story Mediterranean styled resort. A series of arches in the pink stucco entry leads in to a cavernous lobby where San Francisco designer John Dickinson has created an interior of understated elegance. Monochromatic earth colors and natural fabrics are used throughout. The rooms are a bit cozy, but exceedingly comfortable. Wooden shuttered windows overlook the olympic pool where, in the summer, bronzed bodies occupy the rows of white chaises. Spacious tented cabanas can be rented for a day of entertaining.

Adjacent, is the Inn's glamorous European styled luxury spa. Guests can enroll in an individualized program that combines body conditioning, beauty care, massage, herbal cleansing, hydrotherapy and gourmet dining.

Sonoma Mission Inn, Boyes Hot Springs, CA 95416. Telephone (707) 996-1041. Accommodations: 100 rooms. Cards: American Express, Visa, Cart Blanche, Master Charge, Diner's. Spa rates: Advance appointment only. General Facility Pass (Three hours in the evening, 6:30-9:00) $25.00. Five day session: $1500.00. Weekend session: $230.00. Room rates: $105.00 Single or Double Occupancy. Includes use of pool, tennis courts, and Continental breakfast.

Travel Notes: _____
_____
_____

GLEN ELLEN

BELTANE RANCH *Inn*

This classic Victorian ranch boasts a colorful history. It is the former haunt of notorious voodoo queen and Madam, Mammy Pleasant who lavishly entertained her wealthy patrons here during the 1890's. After many years of private ownership, the ranch is again open to the public — strictly for bed and breakfast in this incarnation.

The pastoral 1600 acre ranch is an idyllic retreat. The guest rooms are located on the 2nd floor, each with a fantastic view. An enclosed balcony surrounds the upper story where guests may relax or share a bottle of local wine.

Each room is furnished differently with original period antiques; one features a fireplace and all have ceiling fans. A Continental Breakfast of home grown foods is served.

Beltane Ranch, 11755 Sonoma Hwy. (Hwy 12), Glen Ellen 95442. Telephone: (707) 996-6501. Romms: 3, private bath. Price: $50.00-$75.00. No pets, No cards, No children under 12 years.

KENWOOD

SANTA ROSA

SUGARLOAF RIDGE STATE PARK
Campgrounds

The park is open all year and offers camping, riding and hiking on 25 miles of trails on this 2500-acre site. There are 50 campsites, each with table and benches, fire ring, level tent sites and parking spur. No reservations are accepted. No showers. There are picnic facilities. A newly added 5 mile trail link-up to Mt. Hood allows extensive fair weather hiking.

The park is located midway between Sonoma and Santa Rosa. Turn on to Adobe Canyon Road from Hwy. 12 near Kenwood and proceed four miles to the entrance. The roads are narrow and steep.

Sugarloaf Ridge State Park, 2605 Adobe Canyon Road, Kenwood 95452. Telephone: (707) 833-5712. Camping: $3.00 per night. Picnic: $2.00. Dogs must have rabies certificate. Dogs: $1.00 overnight; day use $.50, must be on leash, not allowed on trails.

LOS ROBLES LODGE *Restaurant, Lodging*

The restaurant at Los Robles Lodge offers a full continental and Western menu. Daily specials (Monday-Thursday) are priced at $7.00. Friday: fresh fish special. Saturdays: prime rib $11.00. Sunday: Southern fried chicken is $7.00.

The Lodge offers ninety rooms, all equipped with king, queen or two double beds, air conditioning, color cable T.V., free movies, radios, coffee, free parking and telephones. Two swimming pools and jacuzzi hot tubs are available to guests.

Los Robles Lodge, 925 Edwards Ave., Santa Rosa. Telephone: (707) 545-6330. Restaurant Hours: Lunch 11:00 a.m.-2:30 p.m. daily; Dinner 5-10 p.m.; Sunday Brunch 10 a.m.-2 p.m. Price range: Lunch $2.50-$7.50; Dinner $7.50-$19.50; Corkage $1.50. Lodging prices start at $35.00-$50.00 per night. Cards: MC, BA, CB, AE, DC. Seating 120.

JUST FOR THE HEALTH OF IT *Spa, Sauna*

After a full day of driving and wine tasting, nothing is more reviving than a visit to Just For The Health Of It. Here visitors may partake of a hot tub and sauna in one of the 17 private suites. Each suite houses a redwood hot tub with four jacuzzi jets, a shower complete with soap and towels, cedar sauna and a dressing area. Light switches are equipped with dimmer and there is a choice of piped in music. Fruit juices and mineral waters may be ordered from the juice bar via intercom system. In addition, a visit to the Kohler Environment is available where you can experience Baja Sun, Spring Showers, Jungle Steam, Tropic Rains and Chinook Winds all in one hour.

Just For The Health Of It Sauna and Hot Tub Experience, Corner of 5th and Davis, Santa Rosa, CA. 95402. Telephone (707) 544-4510. Hours: 11 a.m.-midnight, Sunday thru Thursday; Friday and Saturday 11 a.m.-2 a.m. Rates: $6.00-$7.00 an hour per person. Kohler Environment $20.00 per couple.

FREESTONE

GREEN APPLE INN *Inn*

On the way to the ocean on the Bohemian Highway is this wide spot in the road. Downtown Reestone, consisting of half a dozen antique buildings.

Here two small 1860's houses have been combined into a unique Inn. This cheery lodge has been tastefully refurbished by owners Roger and Rosemary Hoffman.

Guests have free run of the house, the kitchen and all the facilities, including hiking trails into the nearby redwood trees where a crystal clear creek runs through meadows of wildflowers.

A full country breakfast of egg pie, fruit juice, tea and coffee is served.

Green Apple Inn, 520 Bohemian Hwy. Freestone 94572. Phone: (707) 874-2526. Accommodations: 4 rooms with two shared baths. Rates: $48.00-$58.00. Wheelchair access. No cards. Reservations required.

GUERNEVILLE

RIDENHOUR RANCH HOUSE *Inn*

The Ridenhour Ranch House is perched on a hill 1/2 mile before reaching Korbel Winery. The comfortable old ranch home is surrounded by bounteous gardens and overlooks a fine view of the Russian River Valley below. A croquet game is set up on the green lawn waiting only for players. Much of this comfortable country inn remains the same as it was when constructed by lumberman Louis B. Ridenhour in 1906, right down to Ridenhour family portraits in the parlor. One of the few concessions to modernity is the secluded hot tub on the grounds. There are 5 guest rooms at the Ridenhour, two with private baths downstairs and 3 with a single shared bath upstairs. Guests are given free reign of the formal dining room or spacious parlor area. A veranda is ideal for mulling over the days news while imbibing a glass of Russian River area wine. Innkeepers Martha and Bob Satterthwaite serve up a sumptuous continental breakfast of hot nut bread and muffins, cheeses and fresh fruit.

Ridenhour Ranch House Inn, 12850 River Road, Guerneville, CA 95446. Telephone (707) 887-1033. Rooms: 5 - 2 with private baths and hot tub. Rates: $50 - 70. Reservations advised. Cards: Master Charge, Visa.

BODEGA BAY

SEA RANCH

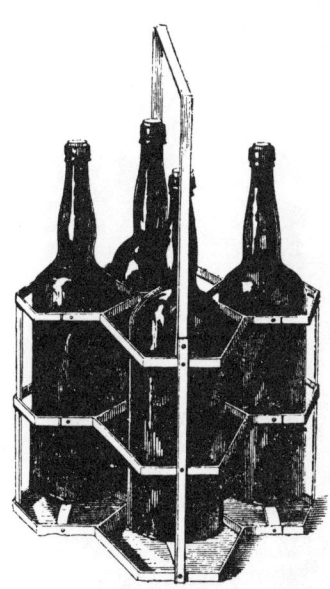

SEA RANCH *Lodging*

Sea Ranch comprises 5200 acres of Sonoma County's most spectacular coastal land. Of this, less than 100 acres are actually occupied by homesites. And what homesites they are: Sea Ranch has received more architectural design awards than any housing development in the world. Every building is constructed of naturally weathering un-painted wood in a style conceived to blend with the natural surroundings. Many of these beautiful second homes are available on a rental basis for the weekend or by the week, providing a unique opportunity to enjoy the seclusion of a private beach front retreat without sacrificing the amenities of civilization. Incidentally, all of the rental homes will accommodate at least two couples very comfortably. For an overnight stay the Sea Ranch Lodge offers to guests spacious, tastefully appointed rooms all with a dramatic ocean view. The lodge is located next to the general store-restaurant complex. Breakfast, lunch and dinner are served at the restaurant seven days a week. The menu here is unpretentious and naturally fresh fish is the specialty. As part of its negotiations to develop this property, Sea Ranch donated 150 acres of rolling meadows and beaches, fronting both the ocean and Gualala River, to the County of Sonoma. This provides an ideal picnicing spot for wine country travelers. Access is on the northernmost edge of Sea Ranch - The Gualala Point County Park exit.

CHANCELLOR RANCH *Inn*

The Chancellor Ranch is located on 700 acres of pristine pasture land overlooking Bodega Bay. It is a meer 3/4 mile from private beaches.

On this working ranch, visitors can expect to share the turf with cattle, sheep and saddle horses. Riding lessons on both horses and ponies are available. Visitors can even bring their own horses if they prefer.

Admittedly the accommodations are rather rustic, but the scenery is the real attraction. Just think of it as a trip to the country — bring the kids, and your faded denims.

On the morning after, guests awaken to a full ranch breakfast complete with fresh eggs and local sausage.

Sea Ranch (north of Jenner, South of Gualala) P.O. Box 44, Sea Ranch, CA 95497, Telephone: (707) 785-2371. Accommodations: Private Homes, Rates: $100 - $202 per/weekend, $279 - $582 per/week. Accommodations: Lodge $52 - $80. Restaurant: Hours Breakfast 8-11 a.m. Lunch 12-3 p.m. Dinner 6-9 p.m. (5-8 Sundays) seven days a week. Cards: Master Charge, Visa, American Express.

Chancellor Ranch, Box 327 Bodega Bay, CA 94923 Phone: (415) 875-3386. Rates $36.00-$49.00 Number of rooms: 5/private baths. Cabin with kitchen, 3 rooms - $150.00 (sleeps 10 comfortably) Cards: VISA, MC. Reservations required.

HEALDSBURG

BELLE DE JOUR *Inn*

Ideally situated for wine touring, Belle de Jour is located a stones throw from Simi Winery. Aptly named, Marie Claire's bed and breakfast Inn is reminiscient of a French country farm house. Raised Redwood boxes spilling over with a profusion of flowers and herbs; peacocks, chickens and goats wander the six acre property; fruit trees fill the air with a pungent scent.

The unpretentious rooms are filled with all sorts of French memorabilia. Overhead fans cool rooms in summer; fireplaces provide winter heating.

A simple breakfast is included in room rates.

Belle de Jour, 16276 Healdsburg Ave., Healdsburg 95446. Telephone: (707) 433-7892. Accomodations: 3 rooms and a private cottage. Rates: $50.00-$60.00. No cards.

GRAPE LEAF *Inn*

The historic residential section of Healdsburg is one of the loveliest and best preserved in all of California. Several blocks from the town square is Lara Salo's gracious home originally constructed in the early 1900's. The home retains its victorian charm with original oriental carpets, light fixtures, brass and crystal. A comfortable and relaxed atmosphere pervades the premises.

Of the four rooms, two have private baths, while two share a bath. Bicycles are available to guests for touring the local country side. A continental breakfast is served.

Grape Leaf Inn, 539 Johnson St., Healdsburg Telephone: (707) 433-8140. Rooms: 4. Rates: $50.00-$60.00. Cat in residence. Wheelchair access. Reservations with deposit. Cards: MC, VISA

HEALDSBURG

RAFORD HOUSE *Inn*

Located on a windy country road outside of Healdsburg, the Raford House is as remote from civilization as you could reasonably expect to get and still be within ten minutes of town. Travelers looking for seclusion will find it here in abundance. This historical landmark sits atop a hill overlooking vistas of orchards and vineyards, but the original hop fields of the 1880's are gone. There are five antique furnished rooms in the Raford House. The 3 downstairs have private baths, exterior entrances, and two have fireplaces. The two upstairs rooms share a single bath. A spacious veranda surrounds the house on three sides, perfect for quiet conversation over continental breakfast. It is a mile walk to the old swimming hole on the Russian River.

Raford House, 10630 Wohler Rd., Healdsburg 95448. Telephone: (707) 887-9573. Rates: $55.00-$65.00. Cards: MC VISA. Reservations suggested. No children or pets.

GEYSERVILLE

HOPE — BOSWORTH HOUSE *Inn*

Built in 1904, this quaint Victorian structure has been painstakingly restored down to the original family photographs which hang on the walls. Even the wallpaper has been custom designed to correctly reflect the period. Both the Hope-Bosworth and the Hope-Merrill house directly across the street were restored and are operated owner Bob and Rosalie Hope. The furnishings here are comfortable and friendly. Three rooms share two baths. Homemade nut breads, fruit juice and coffee cakes are served at the continental style breakfast.

Hope-Bosworth House, 21238 Geyserville Ave., Geyserville 95441. Telephone: (707) 857-3356. Rates: $40.00-$45.00. Reservations with deposit. Number of rooms; 3. No children or pets. Cards: MC VISA.

HOPE — MERRILL HOUSE *Inn*

Of even earlier origin than the Hope-Bosworth House, this structure was originally the local stage coach stop circa 1870. (After the stage line closed down, the coach cross arms were used to build the foundation of the neighboring Hope House). There are six well-appointed bedrooms, each done in antique furnishings which were culled from years of collecting by the owners.

Three rooms share two baths and three have private baths. There is a parlor upstairs with a small outdoor deck featuring a magnificent view of the surrounding countryside. A full country breakfast is included. Both of the Hope houses are within walking distance of local stores.

Hope-Merrill House, 21253 Geyserville Ave., Geyserville 95441. Telephone: (707) 857-3356. Rates: $50.00-$65.00. Cards: MC VISA. Number of rooms: 6. Reservations with deposit. No children or pets.

Travel Notes:

UKIAH

PALACE HOTEL *Inn*

The restoration of Ukiah's Palace Hotel has been a labor of monumental proportion. Original furnishings were combined with contemporary hand worked oak, stained glass and brass to create an aura of turn of the century opulence. Registered as a National Historic Landmark, this three story vine-covered structure is something of a museum of local history. It is said that Black Bart himself often frequented the Saloon and bootleggers hid contraband under the floor tiles. Each cozy room is furnished with original items of Victorian heritage - handmade bedspreads, patchwork quilts and drapes, antique or reproduction furniture and hand-blown light fixtures and lamps. All ninety rooms have individually controlled heat and air conditioning, direct dial phones and private baths. A bouquet of fresh flowers and a bottle of Mendocino wine is placed in each room. Continental breakfasts are included in the room price. Conveniently, Ukiah's finest restaurant, friendliest bar, and liveliest night club are also located in the Palace Hotel.

The Palace Bar & Grill serves breakfast, lunch and dinner daily. The Sunday Brunch is not to be missed, offering a menu of Eggs Benedict, Crab Voisin, Brandied French toast, freshly baked muffins and much more. The wine list features an extensive selection of Mendocino County wines and those not found here are most certainly available at The Mendocino Merchant, a wine and gift shop within the building, boasting over 100 varieties of Mendocino County Wine.

Palace Hotel, 272 North State Street, Ukiah, CA 95482. Telephone (707) 468-9291 (Toll free from No. California (800) 862-4698.) Rooms: 90 Convention & meeting facilities available. Rates: $40 - $90. Reservations recommended. Cards: Master Charge American Express, Diner's. Palace Bar and Grill: Hours: Bar 11:30 a.m. - 2:00 a.m. Breakfast 7:00 - 10:00. Lunch 11:30 - 2:30. Dinner 5:30 - 10:00. Lunch $3.95 - $8.00. Dinner $5.00 - $15.00.

CLOVERDALE

VINTAGE TOWERS *Inn*

It might be argued that Cloverdale is located in the middle of nowhere. Technically this is not true, for Cloverdale is actually the midpoint between two very *decidedly* "somewheres". Halfway between here and there might be a better way of putting it, making this just the right location for a country inn. And not just any old country residence but a full blown 20 room Queen Anne mansion built by Simon Pinschauer in 1903.

Judy and Tom Harwarth spent a great deal of time researching east coast inns before tackling this formidable project. They spent many months painting, remodeling and decorating, creating the appropriate turn of the century atmosphere, but not forgetting such modern amenities as central air-conditiong. Vintage Towers has 3 tower suites, one round, one square, one octagon. Each of the five guest rooms is architecturally unusual and has been restored with period pieces and decorated with individual themes of age and elegance. Breakfast is served between 8 and 10:00.

Vintage Towers, 302 North Main St. Cloverdale, CA 95425. Telephone: (707) 894-4535. Rooms: 5 with shared baths. Prices: $38.00-$58.00. Cards: VISA, MC. No pets or young children.

PHILO   ELK

HENDY WOODS STATE PARK   *Campground*

Thanks to the foresight of foundry-owner, Joshua P. Hendy, some ninety years ago, the magnificent coastal redwoods contained in two groves (Big Hendy Grove and Little Hendy Grove) have been preserved from the loggers. After Hendy sold his land to the Masonite Corporation, this firm also saved the virgin woods from the ax and deeded its 405 acres to the state in 1958. The park was opened to the public in 1963 and further acquisitions increased its size to 601 acres.

Most of the area within Hendy Woods is situated on the north slope of Greenwood Ridge, facing Anderson Valley and the towns of Philo and Boonville. Although the virgin groves of *Sequoia sempervirens,* some of which reach over three hundred feet above the forest floor, are the main attractions, madrones, Douglas firs and California laurels are abundant.

The campgrounds at Hendy Woods are located in a wooded area between Big and Little Hendy groves. Each campsite includes a table, a wood stove, a food locker, and a paved parking space. Restrooms and piped drinking water are nearby. There are no showers.

The picnic area, located on the south bank of the Navarro River, offers the added attractions of swimming and fishing. Steelhead and salmon fishing can be excellent in the fall and winter. A state sport fishing license is required.

Hendy Woods State Park, Star Route 1210, Philo 95466. Telephone: (707) 895-3141. Price: $5.00/night. Number of campsites: 92. Reservations recommended.

HARBOR HOUSE   *Lodging*

The panoramic setting of the Harbor House affords one of the finest views on the North Pacific Coast. A series of megalithic rocks are strewn across a private cove and the relentless throbbing of the sea is nearly hypnotic. The bedroom windows of several rooms at the Harbor House frame this scene. There are five rooms in the main house with four cottages on the grounds. Every room is warmed by a fireplace or Franklin stove and has its own bath. The stately main house was built in 1916 as an executive residence for the Goodyear Redwood Lumber Company and is constructed entirely of virgin redwood taken from the nearby Albion forests. The parlor is reminiscent of that of an elegant private club, with a well-stocked library and record collection at the disposal of the guests. The price of lodging includes a hearty homemade dinner (often featuring the day's fresh fish catch and a country-style breakfast.)

A flight of stairs is neatly tucked into the nearly vertical cliff that extends to the ocean and private cove below the Harbor House. Here guests can beachcomb, by day. A waterfall nearby trickles out of a protrusion of tangled driftwood and creates a fanciful setting.

The pace at the Harbor House is relaxed; the proprietor Trisha Corcoran is friendly and guests are allowed to enjoy their seclusion.

Harbor House, P.O. Box 369, Elk 95432. Telephone (707) 877-3203. Rooms: 5, four cottages. Rates: $90.00-$125.00, full breakfast and dinner included. Wine & beer available. No children, no pets, no credit cards.

Travel Notes:

GUALALA

THE OLD MILANO HOTEL — *Inn*

Gualala is centered in the North Coast's "Banana belt". (admittedly the banana plantings here are rather meagre) There is less fog and more sunshine daily than anyplace else north of Carmel, vastly increasing visitors chances of experiencing good weather in this somewhat unpredictable Climate Zone.

Perched above a secluded private cove, the Old Milano Hotel commands a breathtaking Pacific vista. Lounge chairs are strewn about the lawn, occupied by the occasional guest, watching the endless ocean wash up upon the cliffs below.

Built in 1905 as a railside inn and pub, the hotel has been lavishly refurbished in a style that probable reflects its early history. There are seven rooms at The Old Milano, six of which overlook the ocean. One of these, actually a suite of three rooms, is recommended to honeymooning couples and is appropriately named "La Forza del Destino." Guests may also stay in the "passion Vine" a private vine festooned cottage overlooking the flower garden.

An absolutely first class continental breakfast of fresh fruit, hot home baked bread and locally roasted coffee is delivered to the room. Dinners are available at nearby St. Orres.

Old Milano Hotel, Hwy. 1 (one mile north of Gualala) CA 95445. Telephone: (707) 884-3256. Closed winters. Rooms: 7, 2 private baths. 2 private cottages. Private hot tub. Price Range: $50.00-$110.00. Reservations recommended.

*Travel Notes:*_____
_____
_____
_____
_____
_____

WHALE WATCH — *Lodging*

Right across the street from the Mar Vista on the ocean side of the highway is Whale Watch. It is appropriately named for the winter and spring migrations of grey whales, clearly seen through the ceiling-to-floor plate glass windows of this brand new luxurious redwood lodge. Indeed Whale Watch has perhaps one of the finest views anywhere on the coast. Nearby Fish Rock is the home for hundreds of sea lions, seals and birds; their calls mingled with the sound of pummeling ocean surf provide a truly romantic setting.

Whale Watch, 35100 Highway 1, Anchor Bay, (P.O. Box 127) Gualala 95445. Telephone (707) 884-3667. Units: 2 one bedroom suites, 2 studio units each with full kitchen and fireplace. Rates: $75.00-$90.00 double.

LITTLE RIVER

LITTLE RIVER

LITTLE RIVER INN *Inn*

The Little River Inn accommodations comprise rooms in the main house, the new Hilltop Annex, and some cottage units. The attic rooms of the house are the least expensive, yet the privacy given by the casual cottages, when available, is well worth the higher rate.

The 1853 white frame house standing prominently at the edge of Highway 1 is the original home of lumber and shipping overseer Silas Coombs. Today the Maine-style mansion houses offices, lobby, restaurant, and the few attic rooms, all luxuriously decorated with antiques. For those wishing to experience the sensation of early California, these rooms are recommended.

The cottage units and the contemporary Hilltop Annex which provide the other two types of accommodations are outfitted in eclectic collections of more modern furniture. Every room offers a panoramic view of the sea.

The Inn operates on the European plan. However, the rustic bar and dining rooms where the chef specializes in steaks and seafood are open to the public. A nine-hole golf course attended by a PGA professional and sheltered by eucalyptus trees is available to both guests and passers-by.

Little River Inn, Hwy. 1, Little River 95456. Telephone: (707) 937-5942. Room rates for two: Attic $50.00; Annex $56.00; Suites $64.00-$130.00. Restaurant hours: 7:30 a.m.-2:00 p.m.; Dinner 6:00-10:00 p.m. Price range: Complete dinners $8.50-$18.00. No cards, personal checks accepted. Reservations necessary. Total number of units: 50.

HERITAGE HOUSE *Inn*

Nestled in along the craggy coastline, the historic Heritage House was built in 1877 by the present owner's grandfather, John Dennen. The old barns are long gone, but the newer buildings blend gracefully with both the architecture of the farmhouse and the surrounding landscape.

Most of the accommodations are in the individual cottages scattered throughout the hillside. Each room is decorated differently to reflect the name inspired by early buildings of the area, such as "Schoolhouse," "Stable," "Country Store," and "Ice Cream Parlor." The furnishings include many valued antiques from the immediate vicinity. The Dennens have tried not only to preserve some history and hospitality of an era but also to provide refuge and privacy amid luxurious surroundings.

The room rates are based on a "modified American plan" which includes breakfast and dinner. The lavish breakfasts offer a buffet of fruits, juices and cereals as well as a full American breakfast of bacon and eggs served at the table. Dinners vary nightly on the basis of seasonal availability. Jackets and ties are preferred dinner attire. The wine list is one of the most extensive in the area.

Heritage House, Little River 95456. Telephone (707) 937-5885. Rates: Single $70.00-$128.00; Double $90.00-$148.00. Closes Dec. and Jan. Restaurant hours: Breakfast 8-10 a.m., Dinner 6-8 p.m. Rates: Breakfast $6.00; Dinner $15.00-$20.00. No cards. No pets. Reservations necessary. Units: 62.

Travel Notes:

MENDOCINO

VAN DAMME STATE PARK *Camping, Hiking*

John and Louise Van Damme, a Flemish couple from Belgium, settled at Little River in the 1860's. Their son, Charles, who operated the San Rafael-Richmond Ferry, fondly remembered the old mill town of Little River. His concern that the beach, a favorite picnic spot, remain available for public use, prompted him to purchase forty acres to be used by the people on the coast. At his death in 1930 the land was deeded to the state. Additional acreage was purchased to create Van Damme State Park, now 1826 acres.

The park, in addition to being a good look at the natural world of the coast, reaches back into the canyon, following the long narrow river into the mystical regions of Sword Fern Canyon and the Pygmy Forest. Here thickets of gnarled and lichen-encrusted Mendocino cypress trees, some as old as sixty years, grow just a few feet tall and less than half an inch in diameter. Dwarf Bolander pines range to fifteen feet. The fern growth spreads up from the river on both sides for approximately three miles.

There are now 74 campsites within the park, and some of these are shaded. Restrooms with flush toilets and hot-water showers are nearby. Summer nature programs covering plants and wildlife of the area are a popular feature. There are bicycle trails as well as hiking trails.

Van Damme State Park, c/o Mendocino Area, P.O. Box 940, Mendocino 95460. Telephone: (707) 937-0851. Price: $5.00/night. Reservations recommended. Number of campsites: 74.

MENDOCINO

MacCALLUM HOUSE *Inn, Restaurant*

This splendid three story Victorian was constructed in 1882 by lumber magnate William H. Kelly as a gift for his newlywed daughter Daisy MacCallum.

San Franciscans, William and Sue Norris, purchased the property from the MacCallum family in 1974 complete with all the original furnishings and began transforming it into a charming inn. The Norrises wallpapered the bedrooms with Victorian era prints and covered the antique beds with matching homemade quilts. Even the old greenhouse, gazebo, and water tower have become comfortable guest houses. Bathrooms, as per the boarding house tradition, are communal.

Dining at the MacCallum House is truly a delightful experience. Guests relax around two stone fireplaces while enjoying dishes prepared by chef Robert Parks. The house specialty, rack of lamb, is baked in mustards and herbs and served with Dijon and sherry sauce. When in season the poached salmon filets with Bernaise, almonds and capers is a must. Generous entrees are flawlessly presented with freshly baked bread and sweet butter, tossed salad, two vegetables and potatoes au gratin or rice and mushrooms. A fairly extensive offering of California wines is featured.

MacCallum House, 740 Albion St., P.O. Box 206, Mendocino 95460. Telephone (707) 937-0289. Rates: $34.00-$95.00 double with continental breakfast. Reservations suggested. Rooms 19. Restaurant, (707) 937-5763. Hours: 6-10 p.m. Tues.-Sun. Dinner $8.00-up. Full bar service. Cards: AE, VISA, MC. Dining room open mid-Feb.-Dec.

Travel Notes:

MENDOCINO   GARBERVILLE

MENDOCINO HOTEL *Hotel, Restaurant*

The bright yellow Mendocino Hotel stands out among Main Street's row of historical structures facing the traveler driving north on Highway 1 towards Mendocino. The hotel has been completely rebuilt since its founding in 1878 and redecorated in true Victorian style. The lobby itself is impressive with its authentic antiques and luxuriously colored carpets and chairs. The adjoining bar is similarly decorated to accent the old church window in the ceiling.

The rooms upstairs are small but elegantly and individually decorated in nineteenth century style. Some beds have canopies, and some have heavy carved oak headboards. Although every room has a small washstand, most guests are required to share bathrooms.

Mendocino Hotel, 45080 Main St., Mendocino 95460. Telephone (707) 937-0511. Room rates: $30.00-$150.00, all double occupancy and including breakfast. Restaurant hours: Lunch 11:30 a.m.-2:30 p.m. daily; Dinner 6:00-9:30 p.m. daily. Price range: Lunch $4.00-$6.00; Dinner $9.00-$12.00. Cards: VISA, MC. Reservations advised. Number of rooms: 26.

JOSHUA GRINDLE INN *Inn*

This lovely old Victorian home was built as a wedding gift for Joshua Grindle and his bride in 1879. It was acquired several years ago by Bill and Gwen Jacobson, escapees from the Bay Area. They have completely renovated it since then, paying careful attention to the "New England" heritage of Mendocino.

On the first floor there is a bedroom which boasts an antique four poster bed which overlooks the tree-shaded patio. Upstairs, Joshua Grindle's original bedroom and the Nautical room have views over town and the ocean. Cypress room sports twin, 19th century brass beds.

A hand painted tile fireplace is the center of attraction in the elegant living room where there is always a decanter of sherry and a bowl of fresh fruit available to guests. In the morning, breakfast awaits. Gwen serves homemade bread or rolls, eggs, fruit, coffee and tea in a cheerful sunlit dining room.

Perhaps the nicest thing about this establishment is that it is within walking distance of the shops and restaurants of the town of Mendocino.

Joshua Grindle Inn, 44800 Little Lake, Mendocino 95460. Telephone (707) 937-4143. Accommodations: seven rooms with twin, double & queen size beds, some fireplaces, private bath. No television or phone. Rate: $48.00-$60.00. No cards. Open year round. Children discouraged.

BENBOW INN *Inn*

About a week after your visit to Benbow Inn, a post card will arrive in the mail, "Just a note to say how very nice it was having you with us at Benbow Inn. We hope you enjoy your stay and will return soon to share with us all the wonderful things that we will continue doing to this beautiful Inn." signed Patsy, Chuck and Muffin.

This personal touch is an example of the attention to detail visitors have come to expect from the Benbow Inn. This Tudor Style inn was built in the 1920's.

Breakfast, a buffet, lunch and dinner are served daily, a real necessity in this isolated setting some 200 miles north of San Francisco. Located on a tranquil river setting, the resort features a beach for sunbathing, as well as a private lake for swimming, a nine hole golf course, along with canoeing and hiking in the Redwood forests.

Benbow Inn, 2675 Benbow Drive, Garberville, Ca 95440. Telephone: (707) 923-2124. Rooms: 70. Rates: $30.00-$40.00. Restaurant, full bar service Cards: MC, VISA.

ALEXANDER VALLEY VINEYARDS
   Address: 8644 Hwy. 128, Healdsburg 95448
   Phone: (707) 433-7209
   Hours: 10-5 daily
   Facilities: tasting, sales, tours by appointment
   Winemaker: Harry (Hank) Wetzel, III
   Vineyards: 240 acres
   Volume: 15,000 cases annually

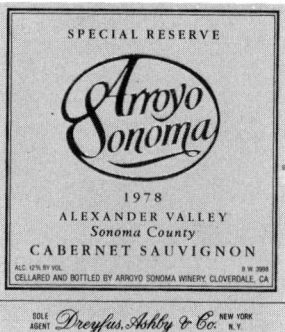

ARROYO SONOMA
   Address: 793 So. Cloverdale Blvd., Cloverdale 95425
   Phone: (707) 894-4295
   Hours: 10:00-5:00 daily
   Facilities: tasting, sales, gifts, tours by appt.
   Winemaker: Tex Sawyer
   Vineyards: 450 acres
   Volume: 53.000 cases annually

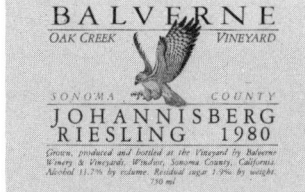

BALVERNE WINERY AND VINEYARDS
   Address: P.O. Box 70, Windsor
   Phone: (707) 433-6913
   Hours: not open to the public
   Facilities: none
   Winemaker: John Kongsgaard and Douglas Nalle
   Vineyards: 250 acres
   Volume: 17,000 cases annually

BELLEROSE VINEYARD
   Address: 435 W. Dry Creek Rd., Healdsburg 95448
   Phone: (707) 433-1637/1120
   Hours: by appt. only
   Facilities: sales, tours by appt. only
   Winemaker: Charles Richard
   Vineyards: 52 acres
   Volume: 3,000 cases annually

BENZIGER FAMILY VINEYARDS
Address: 1883 London Ranch Rd., Glen Ellen 95442
Phone: (707) 996-1066
Hours: by appt. only
Facilities: by appt. only
Winemaker: Mike Benzinger
Vineyards: 60 acres
Volume: 15,000 cases annually

BLUE HERON WINE CELLAR
Address: 71 W. North St., Healdsburg
Phone: (707) 433-1062
Hours: variable
Facilities: not open to the public, at present
Winemaker: Jack Fitzgerald
Vineyards: none
Volume: 2,000 cases annually

BRAREN & PAULI WINERY
Address: 12507 Hawn Creek Rd.,
Potter Valley, 95465
Phone: (707) 526-6440/743-1173
Hours: by appt. only
Facilities: by appt. only
Winemaker: Larry Braren
Vineyards: 40 acres
Volume: 2,000 cases annually

BUENA VISTA WINERY & VINEYARDS
Address: 18000 Old Winery Rd., Sonoma
Phone: (707) 938-1266
Hours: 10-5 daily
Facilities: tasting, sales, self-guided tour
Winemaker: Don Harrison
Vineyards: 700 acres
Volume: 100,000

DAVIS BYNUM
  Address: 8075 Westside Rd., Healdsburg
  Phone: (707) 433-5852
  Hours: 10:30-5 every day
  Facilities: tasting room, sales, tours by appt.
  Winemakers: Davis Bynum & Gary Farrell
  Vineyards: none
  Volume: 20,000 cases annually

CAMBIASO
  Address: 1141 Grant Ave., Healdsberg
  Phone: (707) 433-5508
  Hours: salesroom 10-5 weekdays, 10-4 Sat.
  Facilities: special tours by appt. only
  Winemaker: Bob Fredson
  Vineyards: 38 acres
  Volume: 75,000 cases annually

CHATEAU ST. JEAN
  Address: 8555 Sonoma Highway, Kenwood
  Phone: (707) 833-4134
  Hours: 10-4:30 daily
  Facilities: tasting, sales, tours, picnicking
  Winemaker: Richard Arrowood
  Vineyards: 75 acres
  Volume: 85,000-95,000 cases annually

CLOS DU BOIS
  Address: #5 Fitch St., Healdsburg
  Phone: (415) 456-7310
  Hours: by appt. only
  Facilities: winery and Oak Cellar
  Winemaker: Tom Hobart
  Vineyards: 300 acres
  Volume: 20,000-40,000 cases annually

CORDTZ BROTHERS CELLARS
    Address: 28237 River Rd., Cloverdale
Phone: (707) 894-5245
Hours: 9-5 Mon.-Fri., weekends after May
Facilities: tasting, picnic area
Winemaker: Chuck Ortman, Damian Parker
Vineyards: none
Volume: 6,500 cases

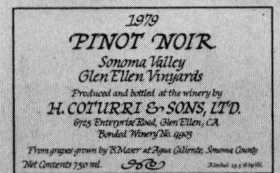

H. COTURRI & SONS, LTD.
    Address: 6725 Enterprise Rd., Glen Ellen
Phone: (707) 996-6247
Hours: not open to the public
Facilities: by appt. only
Winemaker: Tony Coturri
Vineyards: 82 acres
Volume: 1,250 cases annually

CRESTA BLANCA WINERY
    Address: 2399 North State St., Ukiah
Phone: (707) 462-2987
Hours: 9-5 daily except major holidays
Facilities: garden tasting room, guided tours
Winemaker: Gerald Furman
Vineyards: none
Vineyards: co-operative
Volume: 100,000 cases annually

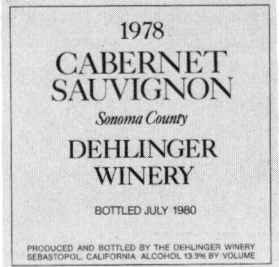

DEHLINGER WINERY
    Address: 6300 Guerneville Rd., Sebastopol
Phone: (707) 823-2378
Hours: 8-5 weekdays
Facilities: call for appt.
Winemaker: Tom Dehlinger
Vineyards: 14 acres
Volume: 8,000 cases

DeLOACH VINEYARDS
Address: 1791 Olivet Rd., Santa Rosa
Phone: (707) 526-9111
Hours: 10-4 daily, except holidays
Facilities: retail sales, picnicking, no tasting
Winemaker: Cecil DeLoach
Vineyards: 140 acres
Volume: 12,000 cases annually

DOMAINE LAURIER
Address: 8075 Martinelli Rd., Forestville
Phone: (707) 887-2176
Hours: by appt. only
Facilities: by appt. only
Winemaker: Stephen Test
Vineyards: 30 acres
Volume: 3,500 casses annually

DONNA MARIA VINEYARDS
Address: 10286 Chalk Hill Rd., Healdsburg
Phone: (707) 838-2807
Hours: not open to the public
Facilities: by appt. only
Winemaker: Charles Illgen
Vineyards: 190 acres
Vineyards: 50
Volume: 10,000 cases annually

DRY CREEK VINEYARD, INC.
Address: 3770 Lambert Brdg. Rd., Healdsburg
Phone: (707) 433-1000
Hours: 10:30-4:30 daily
Facilities: tasting, sales, picnic
Winemaker: David S. Stare
Vineyards: 50 acres
Volume: 30,000 cases annually

EDMEADES
Address: 5500 Calif. St. Hwy. 128, Philo
Phone: (707) 895-3232
Hours: winter 11-5, summer 10-6
Facilities: tasting, tours, sales
Winemaker: Jedediah Steele
Vineyards: 35 acres
Volume: 21,000 cases

FENTON ACRES WINERY
Address: 6192 Westside Rd., Healdsburg
Phone: (707) 433-2305
Hours: not open to the public
Facilities: by appt. only
Winemaker: J. Rochioli, G. O'Connor, J. Brochosfsky
Vineyards: 100 acres
Volume: 3,000 cases

FETZER VINEYARDS
Address: 1150 Bel Arbres Rd., Redwood Valley
Phone: (707) 485-7634
Hours: by appt.; Hopland tasting 9-5 daily
Facilities: tours by appt., tasting at Hopland
Winemaker: Paul Dolan
Vineyards: 160 acres
Volume: 200,000 cases annually

FIELD STONE WINERY
Address: 10075 Ste. Hwy. 128, Healdsburg 95448
Phone: (707) 433-7266
Hours: 10-5 daily
Facilities: tasting, tours by appt., sales, picnic area
Winemaker: Deborah Anne Cutter
Vineyards: 140 acres
Volume: 10,000 cases annually

FISHER VINEYARDS
Address: 6200 St. Helena Road, Santa Rosa
Phone: (707) 539-7511
Hours: by appt. only
Facilities: winery only, no tasting room
Winemaker: Fred J. Fisher
Vineyards: 65 acres
Volume: 4,000 cases annually

FOPPIANO
Address: 12707 Old Rdwd. Hwy., Healdsburg
Phone: (707) 433-7272
Hours: 10-4:30 daily
Facilities: tasting room, picnic ground
Winemaker: Rod Foppiano
Vineyard: 200 acres
Volume: 200,000 cases

GEYSER PEAK WINERY
Address: 22281 Chianti Rd., Geyserville
Phone: (707) 433-6585
Hours: 10-5 daily
Facilities: tasting room, picnic area, hiking trail
Winemaker: Armand Bussone
Vineyards: 625 acres
Volume: 1 million cases

GLEN ELLEN VINEYARDS
Address: 1700 Moon Mtn. Drive, Sonoma, CA 95476
Phone: (707) 829-0398
Hours: none
Facilities: None
Winemaker: Jeff Baker
Vineyards: 60 acres
Volume: 5,000 cases annually

GRAND CRU VINEYARDS
 Address: 1 Vintage Lane, Glen Ellen
 Phone: (707) 996-8100
 Hours: 10-5 weekends only
 Facilities: tasting, sales, picnic grounds
 Winemaker: Robert L. Magnani
 Vineyards: 30 acres
 Volume: 25,000 cases annually

GRAND PACIFIC VINEYARD COMPANY
 Address: 341 San Anselmo Ave., San Anselmo
 Phone: (415) 459-5557
 Hours: 11-5 Mon.-Sat.
 Facilities: tasting, sales, tours by appt.
 Winemaker: Richard Dye
 Vineyards: none
 Volume: 8,000 cases annually

GREENWOOD RIDGE VINEYARDS
 Address: Box 1090 Star Route, Philo
 Phone: (707) 877-3262
 Hours: visitors by appt. only, please
 Facilities: winery
 Winemaker: Allan Green
 Vineyards: 8 acres
 Volume: 1,000 cases

GUNDLACH BUNDSCHU WINE CO.
 Address: 2000 Denmark st., Sonoma
 Phone: (707) 938-5277
 Hours: 12:00-4:30 daily
 Facilities; tours, tasting, sales, picnics, hiking
 Winemaker: John Merritt, Jr.
 Vineyards: 350 acres
 Volume: 25,000 cases annually

HACIENDA WINE CELLARS
Address: 2000 Demnark St., Sonoma
Phone: (707) 938-3220
Hours: 10-5 daily
Facilities: tours by appt., tasting, sales
Winemaker: Steve Mac Rostie
Vineyards: 130 acres
Volume: 20,000 cases annually

HANZELL VINEYARDS
Address: 18596 Lomita Ave., Sonoma 95476
Phone: (707) 996-3860
Hours: not open to the public
Facilities: tours by appt., sales, no tasting
Winemaker: Robert Sessions
Vineyards: 32 acres
Volume: 2.000 cases annually

J.J. HARASZTHY & SON
Address: 14301 Arnold Dr. Glen Ellen, CA 95441
Phone: (707) 996-3040
Hours: 9:00-5:00 Mon.-Fri.
Facilities: no tasting room, tours by appt.
Winemaker: Val Haraszthy
Vineyards: none
Volume: 10,000 cases annually

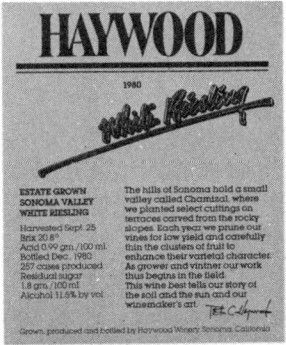

HAYWOOD WINERY
Address: 18701 Gehricke Rd., Sonoma
Phone: (707) 996-4299
Hours: not open to public
Facilities: none
Winemaker: Charles Tolbert
Vineyards: 100 acres
Volume: 4,000 cases

HOP KILN WINERY
    Address: 6050 Westside Rd., Healdsburg
    Phone: (707) 433-6491
    Hours: daily 10-5
    Facilities: tasting, sales
    Winemaker: Dr. L. Martin Griffin, Jr.
    Vineyards: 65 acres
    Volume: 8,000 cases annually

HORIZON WINERY
    Address: 2594 Athena Court, Santa Rosa
    Phone: (707) 544-2961
    Hours: special arrangement only
    Facilities: none for tasting
    Winemaker: Paul Gardner
    Vineyards: none
    Volume: under 1,000 cases

LABEL NOT AVAILABLE AT PRESS TIME

HULTGREN & SAMPERTON WINERY
    Address: P.O. Box 1026, Healdsburg, CA 95448
    Phone: (707) 433-5102
    Hours: not open to the public
    Winemaker: Ed Samperton
    Vineyards: 14 acres
    Volume: 10,000 cases annually

HUSCH VINEYARDS
    Address: 4900 Ca. Ste. Hwy 128, Philo 95466
    Phone: (707) 895-3216
    Hours: 10-5 daily
    Facilities: tours, tasting, sales
    Winemaker: H. A. Oswald III
    Vineyards: 25 acres
    Volume: 6,500 cases annually

IRON HORSE VINEYARDS
Address: 9786 Ross Station Rd., Sebastopol
Phone: (707) 887-2913
Hours: 10-4, Mon.-Fri.
Facilities: by appointment only
Winemaker: Forrest Tancer
Vineyards: 150 acres
Volume: 11,000 cases annually

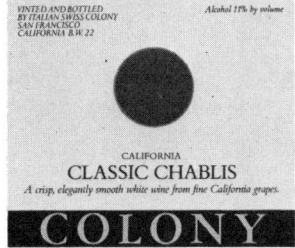

ITALIAN SWISS COLONY
Address: Asti 95425
Phone: (707) 433-2333
Hours: 9-5 daily
Facilities: tours, tasting, sales, picnic area
Winemaker: Thomas Eddy
Vineyards: 600 acres

LABEL NOT
AVAILABLE
AT PRESS TIME

JADE MOUNTAIN WINERY
Address: 1335 Hiatt Rd., Cloverdale 95425
Phone: please write
Hours: not open to the public
Facilities: none
Winemaker: Dr. Douglass Cartwright
Vineyards: 35 acres
Volume: 2,000 cases annually

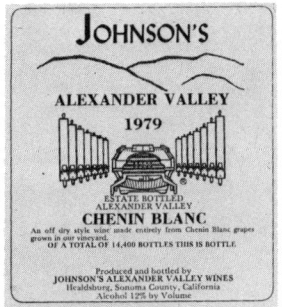

JOHNSON'S ALEXANDER VALLEY WINES
Address: 8333 Ca. Ste. Hwy 128, Healdsburg
Phone: (707) 433-2319
Hours: 10-5 daily: occasional Sun. open house
Facilities: tours, tasting, sales
Winemaker: Tom Johnson
Vineyards: 70 acres
Volume: 10,000 cases annually

JORDAN VINEYARDS
Address: P.O. Box 878, Healdsburg
Phone: (707) 433-6955
Hours: not open to public
Facilities: none available to public
Winemaker: Rob Davis
Vineyards: 250 acres
Volume: 45,000 cases annually

KALIN CELLARS
Address: 61 Galli Dr., Novato
Phone: (415) 883-3543
Hours: by appt. only
Facilities: none
Winemaker: Terrance Leighton
Vineyards: none
Volume: 2,000 cases

KENWOOD VINEYARDS
Address: 9592 Sonoma Hwy., Kenwood
Phone: (707) 833-5891
Hours: 10:00-4:30 daily
Facilities: tasting, sales, tours by appt. only
Winemakers: Dr. R. Kozlowski & M. Lee
Vineyards: 20 owned, 100 under contract
Volume: 55,000 cases

KISTLER VINEYARDS
Address: 2995 Nelligan Rd., Glen Ellen
Phone: (707) 833-4662
Hours: not open to the public
Facilities: none available
Winemaker: Stephen Kistler
Vineyards: 40 acres
Volume: 4,000-6,000 cases annually

F. KORBEL & BROS.
Address: Guerneville 95446
Phone: (707) 887-2294
Hours: 9:45-5:00 daily
Facilities: tours, tasting, sales
Champagne-master: Adolf Heck
Vineyards: 600 acres
Volume: 750,000 cases champagne

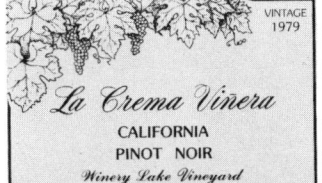

LA CREMA VINERA
Address: P.O. Box 976, Petaluma
Phone: (707) 762-0393
Hours: not open to the public
Facilities: by appt. only
Winemaker: Rod Berglund
Vineyards:
Volume: 2,000 cases annually

LAMBERT BRIDGE
Address: 4085 W. Dry Creek Rd., Healdsburg
Phone: (707) 433-5855
Hours: 8:30-4:30 Mon.-Fri.
Facilities: tours by appt. only
Winemaker: Nick Martin
Vineyards: 90 acres
Volume: 10,000 cases

LANDMARK VINEYARDS
Address: 9150 Los Amigos Rd., Windsor
Phone: (707) 838-9466
Hours: 10-5 Sat. & Sun.; or by appt.
Facilities: tours and sales, picnic area
Winemaker: William R. Mabry, III
Vineyards: 87 acres
Volume: 10,000-15,000 cases annually

LABEL NOT
AVAILABLE
AT PRESS TIME

LAUREL GLEN VINEYARD
    Address: Glen Ellen
    Phone: (707) 546-2875
    Hours: by appt. only
    Facilities: winery only, no tasting
    Winemaker: Patrick Campbell
    Vineyards: 20 acres
    Volume: 2,400 cases annually

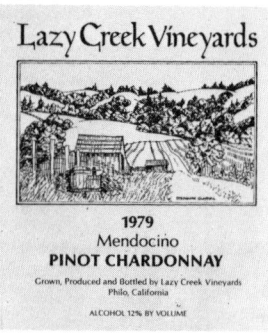

LAZY CREEK VINEYARDS
    Address: 4610 Hwy 128 (P.O. Box 176) Philo, CA 95466
    Phone: (707) 895 3623
    Hours: by appointment only
    Facilities: none
    Winemaker: Johann Kobler
    Vineyards: 20 acres
    Volume: 1,250 cases annually

LE BAY CELLARS
    Address: 26900 Dutcher Creek Rd., Cloverdale
    Phone: (707) 894-3191
    Hours: Wed.-Sun., 10-4
    Facilities: tasting, sales, picnic area
    Winemaker: Douglas Bay Shaffer
    Vineyards: 45 acres
    Volume: 8,000 cases annually

LYTTON SPRINGS WINERY
    Address: 650 Lytton Springs Rd., Healdsburg
    Phone: (707) 433-7721
    Hours: not open to the public
    Facilities: tasting by appt. only
    Winemaker: Walt Walters
    Vineyards: 50 acres
    Volume: 6,000 cases annually

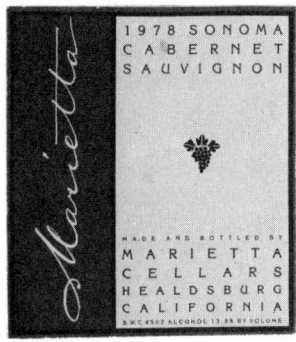

MARIETTA
Address: P.O. Box 1260 Healdsburg, CA
Hours: Closes to public
Facilities: none
Winemaker: Chris Bilbro
Vineyards: none
Volume: 4,000 cases annually

MARK WEST VINEYARDS
Address: 7000 Trenton-Hldsbg. Rd., Forestville
Phone: (707) 544-5813
Hours: weekdays 8-5; Sat. 10-4; Sun by appt.
Facilities: tours & sales only
Winemaker: Joan Ellis
Vineyards: 63 acres
Volume: 8,500 cases annually

MARTINI & PRATI
Address: 2191 Laguna Rd., Santa Rosa
Phone: (707) 823-2404
Hours: 9-4 Mon.-Fri.
Facilities: tasting, sales, no tours
Winemaker: Frank Vanucci
Vineyards: 70 acres
Volume: 1,500,000 gallons annually

MATANZAS CREEK WINERY
Address: 6097 Bennett Valley Rd., Santa Rosa
Phone: (707) 542-8242
Hours: write for appt.
Facilities: sales through mailing list
Winemaker: Merry Edwards
Vineyards: 50 acres
Volume: 3,500 cases annually

MCDOWELL VALLEY VINEYARDS
  Address: 3811. 175, Hopland 95449
  Phone: (707) 744-1053
  Hours: 9:00-4:00
  Facilities: tasting, sales, tours by appt.
  Winemaker: George Bursick
  Vineyards: 360 acres
  Volume: 25,000 cases annually

MILANO WINERY
  Address: 14594 S. Hwy. 101, Hopland 95449
  Phone: (707) 744-1396
  Hours: Thurs.-Sun. 9:00-4:00 P.M.
  Facilities: tasting, sales & tours by appt.
  Winemaker: Jim Milone
  Vineyards: none
  Volume: 8,000 cases annually

MILL CREEK VINEYARDS
  Address: 1401 Westside Rd., Healdsburg
  Phone: (707) 433-5098
  Hours: 10-4 weekdays
  Facilities: sales, tours by appt., no tasting
  Winemaker: James Kreck
  Vineyards: 65 acres
  Volume: 10,000 cases annually

LABEL NOT
AVAILABLE
AT PRESS TIME

MOUNTAIN HOUSE WINERY
  Address: 38999 Hwy. 129, Cloverdale
  Phone: (707) 894-3074
  Hours: by appt. only
  Facilities: tours by appt. only
  Winemaker: Ronald F. Lipp
  Vineyards: 5 acres
  Volume; 2,5000 cases annually

NAVARRO VINEYARDS
  Address: 5601 Ca. Ste. Hwy. 128, Philo
  Phone: (707) 895-3686
  Hours: 10-5 daily
  Facilities: tours by appt., tasting, sales
  Winemaker: Edward (Ted) Bennett
  Vineyards: 35 acres
  Volume: 7,000 cases annually

NERVO WINERY
  Address: P.O. Box 25, Geyserville
  Phone: (707) 857-3417
  Hours: 10-5 daily
  Facilities: tasting, sales, picnic area
  Winemaker: Armand Buzzone

PARDUCCI WINE CELLARS
  Address: 501 Parducci Road, Ukiah
  Phone: (707) 462-3828
  Hours: 9-5 daily
  Facilities: tours, tasting, sales
  Winemakers: John Parducci/Joseph Monostori
  Vineyards: 325 acres
  Volume: 250,000 cases annually

PARSONS CREEK WINERY
  Address: 300 S. State St., Ukiah
  Phone: (707) 462-8900
  Hours: by appt. only
  Facilities: none
  Winemaker: Jess Tidwell
  Vineyards: none
  Volume: 5,000 cases

PASTORI WINERY
Address: 23189 Redwood Hwy., Cloverdale
Phone: (707) 857-3418
Hours: 9-5 daily except holidays
Facilities: tasting, sales
Winemaker: Frank Pastori
Vineyards: 50 acres
Volume: 5,000 cases

PAT PAULSEN VINEYARDS
Address: 25510 River Rd., Cloverdale
Phone: (707) 894-3197
Hours: not open to public
Facilities: none
Winemaker: T. James Mevis
Vineyards: 43
Volume: 1,600 cases

J. PEDRONCELLI WINERY
Address: 1220 Canyon Rd., Geyserville
Phone: (707) 857-3619
Hours: 10-5 daily
Facilities: tasting, sales, no tours
Winemaker: John Pedroncelli
Vineyards: 135 acres
Volume: 125,000 cases annually

POMMERAIE VINEYARDS
Address: 10541 Cherry Ridge Road, Sebastopol
Phone: (707) 823-WINE
Hours: by appt. only
Facilities: none
Winemaker: Ken Dalton
Vineyards: ¾ acre
Volume: 1,200 cases annually

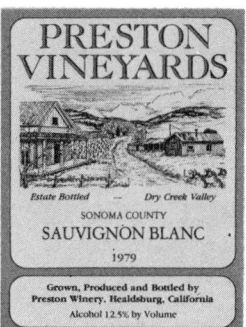

PRESTON VINEYARDS
   Address: 9282 W. Dry Creek Rd.
   Phone: (707) 433-4748
   Hours: not open to public
   Facilities: none
   Winemaker: Louis D. Preston
   Vineyards: none
   Volume: 4,000 cases

A. RAFANELLI WINERY
   Address: 4685 W. Dry Creek Rd., Healdsburg
   Phone: (707) 433-1385
   Hours: by appt. only
   Facilities: sales, no tours or tasting
   Winemaker: Americo Rafanelli
   Vineyards: 25 acres
   Volume: 3,000 cases

RAVENSWOOD
   Address: 5700 Gravenstein Hwy. North
   Phone: (707) 887-2956
   Hours: open by appt. only
   Facilities: storage
   Winemaker: Joel Petterson
   Vineyards:
   Volume:

RICHARDSON VINEYARDS
   Address: P.O. Box 234, Vineburg, CA 95487
   Phone: (707) 938-2610
   Hours: not open to public
   Facilities: not open to public
   Winemaker: Robert Weisheit
   Vineyards: none
   Volume: 2,500 cases annually

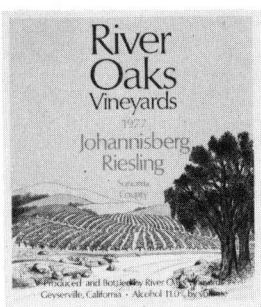

RIVER OAKS VINEYARDS
    Address: Alexander Vly. Rd., Healdsburg
    Phone: (415) 456-7310
    Hours: by appt. only
    Facilities: none
    Winemaker: Frank Woods
    Vineyards: 700 acres
    Volume: not disclosed

RIVER ROAD VINEYARDS
    Address: 6109 Anderson Rd., Forestville
    Phone: (707) 887-1819
    Hours: none
    Facilities: none
    Winemaker: Souverain
    Vineyards: 120 acres
    Volume: 4,000 cases (by Souverain)

ST. FRANCIS VINEYARDS
    Address: 8450 Sonoma Hwy., Kenwood, CA 95452
    Phone: (707) 833-4666
    Hours: 10:00-4:30 daily
    Facilities: tasting, sales, gifts
    Winemaker: Bob Robertson
    Vineyards: 95 acres
    Volume: 12,500 cases annually

SAUSAL WINERY
    Address: 7370 Ca. Ste. Hwy. 128, Healdsburg
    Phone: (707) 433-2285
    Hours: not open to public
    Facilities: none available
    Winemaker: David Demostene
    Vineyards: 150 acres
    Volume: 8,000 cases annually

SEAVIEW WINERY
   Address: P.O. Box 433, Cazadero
   Phone: (707) 847-3469
   Hours: not open to the public
   Facilities: by appt. only
   Winemaker: Daniel E. Wickham, Timothy T. Schmidt
   Vineyards: 14 acres
   Volume: 150 cases

LABEL NOT AVAILABLE AT PRESS TIME

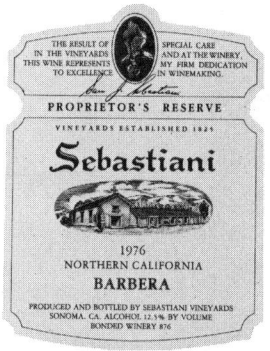

SEBASTIANI VINEYARDS
   Address: 389 Fourth S. E. Sonoma
   Phone: (707) 938-5532
   Hours: 10-5 daily
   Facilities: tours, tasting, sales, museum
   Winemaker: Jim Carter
   Vineyards: 700 acres
   Volume: 3,500,000 cases

SIMI WINERY
   Address: 16275 Healdsburg Ave., Healdsburg
   Phone: (707) 433-6981
   Hours: 10-5 daily
   Facilities: tours, tasting, sales
   Winemaker: Zelma Long
   Vineyards: none
   Volume: 135,000 cases annually by 1985

SODA ROCK WINERY
   Address: 8015 Hwy. 128, Healdsburg
   Phone: (707) 433-1830
   Hours: 10-5 Mon.-Sat. 12-5 Sun.
   Facilities: tasting, tours by appt., sales, pic. area
   Winemaker: Charles Tomka Sr.
   Vineyards: 4 acres, 35 leased
   Volume: 8,500 cases annually

SONOMA VINEYARDS
Address: 11455 Old Redwood Hwy., Windsor
Phone: (707) 433-6511
Hours: 10-5 daily
Facilities: tours by appt., tasting, sales
Winemaker: Rodney D. Strong
Vineyards: 1204 acres
Volume: 500,000 cases annually

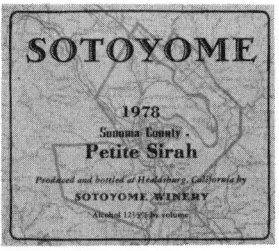

SOTOYOME WINERY
Address: 641 Limmerick Lane, Healdsburg
Phone: (707) 433-2001
Hours: by appt. only
Facilities: tours, tasting, sales
Winemaker: Bill Chaikin
Vineyards: 7.5 acres
Volume: 2,500 cases annually

SOUVERAIN CELLARS
Address: 400 Souverain Rd., Geyserville
Phone: (707) 433-8281
Hours: 10-5 daily
Facilities: tours, tastings, sales, art showings, restaurant
Winemaker: Bob Muller
Vineyards: 10 acres
Volume: 500,000 cases

ROBT. STEMMLER WINERY
Address: 3805 Lambert Brdg. Rd., Healdsburg
Phone: (707) 433-6334
Hours: by appt. only
Facilities: sales, no tours or tasting
Winemaker: Robert Stemmler
Vineyards: 3 acres
Volume: 4,000 cases

JOSEPH SWAN VINEYARDS
  Address: 2916 Laguna Rd., Forestville 95436
  Phone: (707) 546-7711
  Hours: not open to the public
  Facilities: none available
  Winemaker: Joseph Swan
  Vineyards: 10 acres
  Volume: 2,000 cases annually

TOPOLOS AT RUSSIAN RIVER VINEYARDS
  Address: 5700 Gravenstein Hwy. No., Forestville
  Phone: (707) 887-2956
  Hours: Wed.-Sun., 11-5. Winter, 11-5, Fri.-Sun.
  Facilities: tasting, restaurant. Tours by appt. only.
  Winemaker: Michael J. Topolos
  Vineyards: 75 acres
  Volume: 7,500 cases annually

TOYON VINEYARDS
  Address: 71 W. North St. Ste. T, Healdsburg
  Phone: (707) 433-6847
  Hours: 9-4:30 daily
  Facilities: 11,700 total storage capacity
  Vineyards: 5 acres
  Volume: 5,000 cases annually

TRENTADUE VINEYARDS
  Address: 19170 Redwood Hwy., Geyserville
  Phone: (707) 433-3104
  Hours: 10-5 daily
  Facilities: tasting, sales, gift shop, picnicking
  Winemakers: Leo & Victor Trentadue
  Vineyards: 200 acres
  Volume: 15,000 cases annually

TYLAND VINEYARDS
Address: 2200 McNab Ranch Rd., Ukiah
Phone: (707) 462-1810
Hours: 10-4
Facilities: tasting, sales, picnic area, tours, gifts
Winemaker: Don Baker
Vineyards: 300 acres
Volume: 300 cases annually

VALLEY OF THE MOON WINERY
Address: 777 Madrone Rd., Glen Ellen
Phone: (707) 996-6941
Hours: 10-5 daily except Thursday
Facilities: tasting, sales, no tours
Winemaker: Harry Parducci & Otto Toschi
Vineyards: 260 acres
Volume: 90,000

WEIBEL CHAMPAGNE VINEYARDS
Address: 7051 N. State St., Ukiah
Volume: 750,000 cases annually

WM. WHEELER VINEYARDS
Address: 130 Plaza St., Healdsburg, 95448
Phone: (707) 433-8786
Hours: by appt. only
Facilities: by appt. only
Winemaker: Bill Arbios
Vineyards: 30 acres
Volume; 8,000 now to 15,000 later

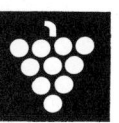

WILLOWSIDE VINEYARDS
   Address: 3349 Industrial Drive, Santa Rosa
   Phone: (707) 544-7504
   Hours: by appt. only
   Facilities: by appt. only
   Winemaker: Berle Beliz
   Vineyards: 24 acres
   Volume: 7,000 cases annually

WOODBURY WINERY
   Address: 32 Woodland Ave., San Rafael
   Phone: (415) 454-2355
   Hours: by appt. only
   Facilities: sales, tours, & tasting
   Winemaker: Russell Woodbury
   Vineyards: none
   Volume: 4,000 cases annually

VINTAGE IMAGE

CATALOGUE

Thank you for buying this Vintage Image book. We hope you are enjoying it and have found it useful. Over the years, we at Vintage Image have strived to bring to our customers products that are both informative and of intrinsic aesthetic value, for it is our belief that art and wine are inextricably interwoven. Because Vintage Image is such a small company, we seek your indulgence with our seemingly slow pace. In truth, we are feverishly working to produce new and exciting projects for your discernment. This year marks the scheduled completion of our California Wine Book Series - All four volumes - Napa Valley, Sonoma & Mendocino, Central Coast, South Coast & Inland Valleys. As is our custom, so as to be all inclusive and up-to-date, we will revise each book in its entirety at least bi-annually (more often if needed).

We are working on a number of other unique wine-oriented projects at our studios here in the Napa Valley and would like you to stop by and visit or send for our free catalogue.

VINTAGE IMAGE, 1335 Main St., St. Helena, CA 94574